S0-ATZ-449

Our Lord Jesus Christ gave His church a great commission to make disciples who will mature and reproduce their kind. In this truly important book Bob McNabb provides committed Christians with practical lessons on how we can more effectively fulfill our calling. To be sure there are many practical books on disciple-making, but this volume is unique. McNabb employs Scripture, original research and many years of personal experience to produce work that I think will emerge as companion volume to Robert E. Coleman's classic *The Master Plan of Evangelism*. Indeed, I intend to make it required reading for all of my students.

~ **Lyle W. Dorsett**, Billy Graham Professor of Evangelism, Beeson Divinity School, Samford University

Bob McNabb has done an excellent job at laying out the keys to spiritual multiplication. His research on which practices are effective and which are not is eye-opening and very helpful. Every pastor and Christian leader needs to study this book and implement the applicable features. What a difference this can make in an organization's or an individual's spiritual impact.

~ **Dr. Frank Barker**, Pastor Emeritus, Briarwood Presbyterian Church

Bob McNabb has given disciples of Jesus a clear, practical guide toward being faithful to the Great Commission and making more disciples of Jesus. Full of insightful research, clear thinking, and years of experience, pastors looking to establish a discipleship culture in their churches would especially benefit from McNabb's work.

~ **Matt Carter**, Pastor of Preaching & Vision at The Austin Stone Community Church and co-author of *The Real Win*

Experts in the field of persuasion are now teaching that successful models are the most effective resources for influencing others. Thanks, Bob, for facing up to the fact that some models are not successful and providing us with well-documented and researched successful models for every aspect of spiritual multiplication. You have given us a handbook, an encyclopedia, which will increase the momentum of spiritual multiplication, not only in our generation, but generations to come.

~ **Jim Downing**, Former Deputy President and Chairman of the Board, The Navigators

Bob McNabb writes about discipleship from decades of international experience. The lessons in the book have been forged in the real world and have indelibly shaped my own life and ministry. 'The harvest is plentiful but the laborers are few.' Bob has pointed us back to Jesus' model of multiplying laborers for the harvest. If you are serious about making and multiplying disciples in the real world, *Spiritual Multiplication in the Real World* is a must read.

~ **Tom Mullis**, Director of Strategy & Leadership Development, United World Mission

We've all heard the grandiose theories of how discipling one person who disciples someone else will eventually fill the entire world with new disciples. But reality tells us something entirely different, and we wonder why this isn't happening. Bob McNabb exposes some of the discipleship multiplication myths while providing statistically backed research on what effectively make disciples who make disciples. I was encouraged, for example, by McNabb's discovery that evangelism training doesn't correlate with evangelistic effectiveness. Rather, joining a team that is practicing evangelism makes all the difference. He also found that group discipleship is more effective than the one-on-one type, and of course, Jesus used the group method to prepare his own disciples. McNabb provides many more principles, so you'll need to read the book to benefit from Bob McNabb's excellent research.

~ **Joel Comiskey**, Ph.D., President of Joel Comiskey Group

Recovering the church's responsibility for the Great Commission is at the very heart of all that Bob does and has written here. Not only is it the Church's responsibility as a whole, it is my responsibility and your responsibility as followers of Jesus. However, the gap often lies between what I know I *should* do, and actually making it a part of my life. *How do we bring people from unbelief to maturity and even leadership for the Kingdom?* Bob has helped many to answer that question, and he can help you. For those that want to follow Jesus' command to make disciples, you will find his book both captivating and practical. May it be used in your life to inspire and enable you to live and lead like Jesus.

~ **Bryan Brown**, Director of Leader Development, Perimeter Church/Campus Outreach

Bob McNabb has given us an outstanding study of what the Bible has to say about spiritual multiplication. His reflections are firmly rooted in the teachings of the Old and New Testaments and demonstrate that every follower of Christ should be devoted to making more and more disciples of Jesus. But more than this, Bob has given us practical advice that stems from many years of serving the cause of Christ. This is the work of a man who is so devoted to spreading the Gospel so that more and more people may worship and serve the one true God. I highly recommend it to every pastor and lay person.

~ **Richard Pratt**, Ph.D., President, Third Millennium Ministries

McNabb has mastered the art of making disciples. In this book, he passes along what he has learned as a caring, humble, and gifted coach. Every chapter is filled with wisdom. So I say, begin. Join with others who have a go-for-it attitude. There will be failures. Don't give up. You can make disciples. You can make disciple-makers. You and your friends can change the world.

~ **Bob Blincoe**, Ph.D., US Director, Frontiers

Bob McNabb is a practitioner in the area of life-on-life ministry. His "practices" grow from his study of scripture; in particular the life and ministry of Jesus. His experience and research contained in this book will help you practice the lifestyle God invites every Christian to be a participant in for the multiplying of disciple-makers of Christ.

~ **Mike Hearon**, Global Leadership Team, Campus Outreach

Bob McNabb has created a very practical, and easy to understand guide to discipleship. His depth of understanding comes from personal experience, and the stories he shares from his own ministry are very motivating and encouraging. They show how any believer can be engaged in spiritual multiplication.

~ **Enoch Yuttasak Sirikul**, Chairman, Thailand Campus Crusade for Christ, Chairman, Executive Committee of Evangelism and Church Growth in Thailand

SPIRITUAL
MULTIPLICATION
IN THE
REAL WORLD

Why some disciple-makers reproduce when others fail.

BOB MCNABB

Scripture quotations are from The Holy Bible, English Standard Version® (ESV®), copyright © 2001 by Crossway, a publishing ministry of Good News Publishers. Used by permission. All rights reserved. Italics found in Scripture quotations reflect the author's own emphasis.

Copyright © 2013 Robert C. McNabb

All rights reserved. No part of this publication may be reproduced or transmitted in any form or by any means—electronic, mechanical, digital, photocopy, recording, or any other—except for brief quotations in printed reviews, without the permission from the publisher.

ISBN 978-1-942374-00-8

To pastors, campus ministers,

and graduates who long to see disciples

reproduce in the "real world."

CONTENTS

ACKNOWLEDGEMENTS

This book was completed only with the help of many friends, co-workers, and family members. Because so many different people helped in the distribution of surveys, statistical analysis of data, prolonged discussions about the meaning of our findings, writing, editing, and theological and ministry principles review process, I will often speak in the first person plural when I refer to our research findings.

Before acknowledging anyone else, I want to say thank you, Jesus, for your unconditional love and the sustaining grace that you give me to live each day. And thank you, Lord, for the following people who were so helpful to me in researching and writing this book:

My beautiful wife Susan and daughters Abigail, Jessica, and Ashley were great encouragers and very understanding with me as I needed time alone to write.

Dr. Jay McCollum and Curtis Tanner invested their lives in me and helped me understand what it means to multiply myself spiritually.

Jim Jager was generous with his resources at New South Research.

Susanna Pearce was such a servant to set up the data in SPSS and to answer all my questions about how to use the software.

Dr. Robert Coleman, Dr. Frank Barker, Mike Hearon, and Alan Love were all gracious enough to grant me interviews while I was in the process of defining the research questions.

Todd Pevey was an incredible help in the data collection process and in just about every other aspect of the research as well.

Will Groben gave critical feedback during the data analysis stage as well as helpful editorial comments throughout.

Drs. Howard Eyrich, Rick Higgins, and Junias Venugopal gave me helpful feedback during the research process. I appreciate their tremendous pastoral spirit while encouraging rigorous research standards.

Jim Doggett buoyed my spirit often with his friendship, interest in the study, and willingness to discuss and refine the application of ministry principles.

Camille Platt, Christina Jerrett, Joanna Reynolds, Sharon Stebbins, Paul Sewell, and Hailey Prescott all gave very helpful feedback on the manuscript.

Dr. Todd Ahrend deserves special recognition for the invaluable input he gave on making this book more readable.

Dozens of unnamed friends, disciple-making team members, and staff helped by distributing surveys, testing out these principles in their ministries, and giving feedback on the manuscript.

More than four hundred survey respondents helped all of us understand what it takes to see spiritual multiplication happen in the real world.

Thank you to all of you who helped, and may God multiply your lives for his glory.

FOREWORD

The population of our world now tops seven billion. Contemplating our responsibility to make disciples of so many can be overwhelming. How can we possibly present a loving and relevant witness to such multitudes? The Master had a plan to do just that. The principle behind it is the same one that populated the earth—exponential multiplication. A careful study of the life of Christ reveals a deliberate strategy to raise up multiplying disciples. A spiritually reproducing Christ-follower holds the same potential for explosive fruitfulness as a seed which can produce thirtyfold, sixtyfold, even a hundredfold what is sown.

With the needs of the world so great and the stakes so high, we cannot afford to just maintain the status quo. Merely adding members to church rolls will not do. Our mandate is to bring the Gospel to every tongue, tribe, and nation. This translates into making disciples who will become disciple-makers.

That is why it is a pleasure to commend this volume. Bob McNabb has been seeking to measure his life by the Great Commission for over thirty years. More to the point, he has a passion to help other followers of Christ multiply laborers for the harvest. This has led to a careful study of the Scriptures and extensive research asking the question of why some workers reproduce and others fail.

His findings presented here come from real world situations, and have been field tested. While the author offers many fresh insights into different aspects of the discipling process, one central theme emerges—discipling happens more naturally when doing it with others; it is a team sport. I appreciated, too, the observation that evangelism and discipleship flow together, and a person does not have to attain the far reaches of sanctification before getting started.

Inspiring stories, practical worksheets, and accompanying guidebooks are provided to assist readers on their own journey of spiritual reproduction. It is my hope that believers everywhere will band together in the Name of Christ to apply the timeless principles taught in these pages, hastening the day when the knowledge of the glory of God will cover the earth as the waters cover the sea.

This is the day we long for. Speeding its coming through spiritual multiplication is our privilege.

Robert Coleman, Ph.D.
Distinguished Senior Professor of Evangelism and Discipleship
Gordon-Conwell Theological Seminary

FOREWORD

Ordinary people with extraordinary power preaching, praying, giving, and suffering for the spread of the gospel.

This is the picture of the early church that we see on the pages of the New Testament. A small band of twelve men responded to a life-changing invitation: "Follow me, and I will make you fishers of men" (Matthew 4:19). In the days to come, they watched Jesus, listened to him, and learned from him how to love, teach, and serve others the same way that he did. Then came the moment when they saw him die on a cross for their sins, only to rise from the dead three days later. Soon thereafter, he gathered them on a mountainside and said to them, "All authority in heaven and on earth has been given to me. Therefore go and make disciples of all nations, baptizing them in the name of the Father and of the Son and of the Holy Spirit, and teaching them to obey everything I have commanded you. And surely I am with you always, to the very end of the age" (Matthew 28:18-20). Just like Jesus had said from the beginning, these followers would now become fishers of men. His authoritative commission would become their consuming ambition.

Not long thereafter, they gathered together with a small group of others, about 120 in all, and they waited. True to his promise, Jesus sent his Spirit to every one of them, and immediately they began proclaiming the gospel. In the days to come, they scattered from Jerusalem to Judea to Samaria to the ends of the earth, and within one generation, they grew to over four hundred times the size they were when they started.

How did this happen?

The spread of the gospel in the book of Acts took place primarily because ordinary people empowered by an extraordinary presence were proclaiming the gospel everywhere they went. To be sure, God did appoint well-known apostles like Peter, John, and Paul for certain positions of leadership in the church. Yet it was anonymous Christians (i.e., not the apostles) who first took the gospel to Judea and Samaria, and it was unnamed believers who founded the church at Antioch, which became a base for mission to the Gentile world. It was unidentified followers of Jesus who spread the gospel throughout all of Asia. Disciples were made and churches were multiplied in places the apostles never went. The Good News of Jesus spread not just through gifted preachers, but through everyday people whose lives had been transformed by the power of Christ. They were going from house to house and in marketplaces and shops along streets and travel routes, leading people to faith in Jesus on a daily basis.

This is how the gospel penetrated the world during the first century: through self-denying, Spirit-empowered disciples of Jesus who were making disciples of Jesus. Followers of Jesus were fishing for men. Disciples were making disciples. Christians were not known for casual association with Christ and his church; instead, they were known for complete abandonment to Christ and his cause. The great commission was not a choice for them to consider, but a command for them to obey. And though they faced untold trials and unthinkable persecution, they experienced unimaginable joy as they joined with Jesus in the advancement of his Kingdom.

I want to be part of a movement like that. I want to be part of a people who really believe that we have the Spirit of God in each of us for the spread of the gospel through all of us. I want to be a part of a people who are gladly sacrificing the pleasures, pursuits, and possessions of this world because we are living for treasure in the world to come. I want to be part of a people who are forsaking every earthly ambition in favor of one eternal aspiration: to see disciples made and churches multiplied from our houses to our communities to our cities to the nations.

This kind of movement involves all of us. Every single follower of Christ fishing for men. Every single disciple making disciples. Men and women from diverse backgrounds with different gifts and distinct platforms making disciples and multiplying churches through every domain of society in every place on the planet. This is God's design for his church, and disciples of Jesus must not settle for anything less.

This kind of movement is what this book is all about. I am grateful to God for His grace in Bob McNabb. I have had the pure joy of watching the way he lives out what he has written here, both in Birmingham, Alabama, and around the world. Seeing Bob's life and reading this book, I am overjoyed when I think about what might happen if men and women not only read this book, but put it into practice. What if followers of Christ in local churches were actually making disciples of Jesus who were making disciples of Jesus, all with the ultimate intent of reaching people and peoples who still haven't heard of Jesus? Oh, I pray that God in His grace might see fit to bless this book in your life and in the lives of countless others toward that end.

David Platt, Ph.D.
President of the International Mission Board
Southern Baptist Convention

Part 1

The Vision and Challenges of Spiritual Multiplication

Chapter 1

STARS AND SAND

When was the last time you had a vacation? How about taking one with me right now in your mind? Let's go to one of my favorite places. It's a tiny island in the south of Thailand called Koh Ngai, or as my wife likes to call it, "Gilligan's Island." She likes to sit on the beach and read while I spearfish for our dinner. The reason I invited you here, however, is not for the fishing. I asked you to join me on the beach because it is my favorite place to talk with people about spiritual multiplication. Let's make it nighttime. We have just finished eating the grouper and lobster we caught today. As you sit down, take off your shoes and get some sand between your toes. Listen to the waves come in as you tilt your head back. Take a good long look at the dizzying array of stars sprinkled across the universe. Now that you're comfortable, let me ask you a few questions.

1. Do you believe God wants to multiply your life and make your spiritual descendants as numerous as the stars in the sky and the sand under your feet?
2. What are you *specifically* asking God to do through your life?
3. How many men or women are you asking God to equip through you as multiplying disciples?
4. How many nations are you asking God to impact through you?

If you can't answer these questions succinctly and immediately, without hesitation, I wonder if you are really trusting God the way he wants you to.

Later in this book I want to share with you some principles of ministry that will help you see fruit in disciple-making. That will all be in vain, however, if you don't really believe that God wants to multiply *your* life. Maybe you can believe he wants to use someone else in amazing ways. But can you believe he actually wants to bless the nations through *your* life?

Hear those waves come crashing in? Listen to them as you reflect on what the book of James says about the importance of faith.

> But let him ask in faith, with no doubting, for the one who doubts is like a wave of the sea that is driven and tossed by the wind. For that person must not suppose that he will receive anything from the Lord; he is a double-minded man, unstable in all his ways. (James 1:6-8)

If you're like me, those four questions and James' comments make you feel short on the kind of faith you need. Since faith comes from hearing the Word, how about looking with me in Scripture at God's cosmic purpose and your role in it? I'm pretty sure that when you see the centrality of multiplication in God's global plan and his firm commitment to blessing the nations through his children, your heart will be encouraged. You will believe more fully that he can use even someone as broken as you or me to accomplish astonishing things.

BORN TO MULTIPLY

"The two most important days
in your life are the day you are born
and the day you find out why."[1]

As a senior in high school, I began to wrestle with what I should do with the rest of my life. Something seemed terribly wrong with the prospect of spending my days working and my evenings watching T.V. There had to be more to life than that, I reasoned. Questions about life and my future eventually led to my salvation. I was now promised an unimaginable paradise in heaven. So why did God leave me here on earth? Why was I born again and left on this planet? Why is anyone born on earth?

Adam and Eve were created to know God and multiply his image bearers throughout the earth.

> So God created man in his own image, in the image of God he created him; male and female he created them. And God blessed them. And God said to them, "Be fruitful and multiply and fill the earth…" (Genesis 1:27-28)

Multiply they did. Jim Downing, former Deputy President of the Navigators, a discipleship focused ministry, made the following comment in a recent email he sent me:

> "I once wondered if Adam and Eve, in their old age, ever tried to figure how many descendants they had. According to my research, using the information in the Bible, the number was more than two million."

Because sin entered the world and marred God's image in man, physical multiplication alone will not fill the earth with God's image bearers. Those who are born again in Christ must multiply spiritually and saturate the world with God's glorious image. It is in them that the image of God is being restored and through them that his glory will be more fully known on earth as his Spirit works in them. As Paul tells the Corinthians:

> And we all, with unveiled face, beholding the glory of the Lord, are being transformed into the same image from one degree of glory to another. For this comes from the Lord who is the Spirit. (2 Corinthians 3:18)

When Jesus ascended to heaven, he didn't take his disciples with him. He had something he wanted them to do here first—go and multiply disciples in all nations. You and I are no different. We were born again to multiply. Our salvation doesn't just deliver us from our sins. It also sets us free from living meaningless lives. That's good news! That's the gospel.

Through spiritual multiplication, your limited years on earth can have an exponential and enduring influence on eternity. When we focus our personal ministries on raising up disciples-makers and not just disciples, our impact widens and continues through others even long after we are gone. Spiritually reproducing in a few now could result in impacting millions, even billions for eternity.

Sometimes I imagine sitting at heaven's gate and greeting newcomers. Leaning back in my chair and sipping lemonade, I give high fives to those I have led to Christ as they come in. After that, those they have led to Christ arrive, and I give them, my spiritual grandchildren, high fives as they enter. Then come my great-grandchildren, my great-great-grandchildren and so on with ever growing numbers. Am I crazy for dreaming about this happening? I'm not so sure about the chair and lemonade part, but I'm in good company in hoping to see those I've impacted when I am with the Lord. The apostle Paul says, "For what is our hope or joy or crown of boasting before our Lord Jesus at his coming? Is it not you? For you are our glory and joy" (1 Thessalonians 2:19-20). This could be your joy too!

REALITY CHECK

Spiritual Multiplication: *Sounds good on paper, but will it actually work in the "real world"?*

The Norden bombsight was marketed as *the* tool to win the Second World War. It was a mechanical computer that calculated a bomb's trajectory based on current flight conditions. Claims were made that it could drop a bomb into a pickle barrel from 20,000 feet. By the end of World War II, the United States had invested $1.5 billion into the Norden's development.

In practice, the Norden never managed to produce accuracies remotely like those of which it was theoretically capable. Both the U.S. and Royal Air Forces used the Norden and experienced extremely poor results. What had looked so promising on paper and worked well in a laboratory failed to yield the desired results in actual battle. Could spiritual multiplication, when attempted in the "real world," be doomed to fail, too? Maybe it can happen in a semi-controlled environment like a college campus or military base, but can it actually happen at my office?

I started asking these questions after seeing many students, who were very fruitful disciple-makers while in college, graduate and bear little fruit. I began to wonder if it is possible to multiply one's life spiritually no matter the context. If so, what is involved in that process? Does it matter what kind of church a person attends? What kind of lifestyle would be needed? Does the type of job one works or where one lives matter? Is there a certain approach to evangelism that yields more fruit? Should the use of materials in discipling be encouraged or discouraged? *Why do some people successfully multiply their lives year after year while others, who have received similar training, flounder and fail to reproduce?* These questions troubled me for years.

In the following chapters, I share the answers I discovered through Bible study, surveying hundreds of disciple-makers, and over thirty years of personal involvement in the process of spiritual multiplication. I'll be the first to admit that my answers aren't perfect. I'm definitely still learning. But, as you will see, what I will share is plainly taught in God's infallible word and illustrated through research findings. You will gain a confidence as I have, that if you apply these principles, spiritual multiplication in the real world is not only possible, but it's inevitable.

NO PLAN B

It's always a good idea to have a backup plan, right? I got my pilot's license when I was in high school. One of the things they teach you when learning to fly cross-country trips is to always select an alternative airport destination in case there is bad weather or some other problem with your plan A. I certainly saw the value in this one morning when I was flying my father from west Florida to a business appointment on the east coast. As we approached our intended airport, I radioed the control tower and received no answer. I tried again and again with the same result. After surveying my instrument panel, I realized that the plane's generator had quit working and the remaining power in the dying battery was not enough to get our signal to the tower. Immediately I switched to my plan B, an uncontrolled airport nearby where I could land without talking to a tower operator. It's good to have a backup plan ready in case your first plan doesn't work out.

So what's Jesus' backup plan? What if his disciples failed in their attempts to multiply? Is there an alternate plan we can switch to if we find ourselves failing at spiritual multiplication? Perhaps there are some other cool programs we could implement. The fact is there are no other options. God has only one plan of how to fill the earth with his children. It is the same plan that he used to populate the earth—multiplication. Since his commitment to it is so absolute, he developed no other strategy. This plan is so firmly established throughout Scripture, it deserves to be considered a doctrine.

THE DOCTRINE OF MULTIPLICATION

Over the years I have read quite a few books on theology and dozens of doctrinal statements. One frequent omission from these is the clear teaching of Scripture on God's intent to build a people for himself through the spiritual multiplication of his children. This teaching is so central and pervasive in Scripture that I think we should speak of it as the Doctrine of Multiplication. It might be a stretch to speak of it as a doctrine if we just found it in a verse or two. But we find this teaching repetitively reinforced in Scripture in all of the following ways:

- It was in the design and commission of creation.
- It was central to God's covenant with Abraham.
- It was reconfirmed to Abraham's descendants Isaac, Jacob, David, and the Levitical priests.
- It was used by Moses to persuade the Lord to spare the Israelites from destruction.
- It was modeled by Jesus and his apostles.
- It was commanded by Jesus in the New Testament.
- It was promised as a reward to all faithful disciples of Christ.
- It was displayed as accomplished in the book of Revelation.

From Genesis to Revelation, the Bible is a book about God's desire and plan to spread the glory of his own image by multiplying a people for himself. Initially, physical and spiritual multiplication were integrated in one process. As a result of sin and mankind's spiritual death, this single process was ripped apart and became two. While this book focuses on the process of spiritual multiplication, it must be noted that our doctrine of multiplication is rooted in the perfection of God's original design for man. Through seeing God's design, we understand what is in the heart of God, and from there we build our theology of multiplication.

MAN'S COMMISSION SINCE CREATION

From the beginning of the human race, it has been understood that God has a desire to have a people for himself. His method for reaching this end was made clear in the command he gave Adam and Eve, "Be fruitful and multiply…" (Genesis 1:28). This command was given before the fall. All that flows out of a perfect and holy God is *by necessity* perfect and holy. He perfectly fitted mankind for the task of multiplication and hardwired into Adam and Eve the desire to carry out the charge. He gave them a mind and heart that would find deep satisfaction in seeing the process through to the third generation and beyond. God intended for parenthood to be considered a gift from the Lord and grandparenthood to be an even greater joy.[2] While it is wonderful to have physical children, anyone who has spiritual children and grandchildren will tell you of the unspeakable joy it also brings.[3] Multiplication, physical or spiritual, is not a burden to be endured, but a privilege to be enjoyed. God designed you in such a way as to desire it and delight in it.

GOD'S PROMISES

When God promised to bless Abraham, a significant part of that blessing was the proliferation of his descendants. Multiplication is not just a duty of man, it is a promised blessing. Let's look now at some of the instances of God giving and reiterating this promise, not just to Abraham, but to all who share in the faith of Abraham as well.

ABRAHAM

The Lord chose to create a people for himself through the descendants of Abraham, so he made a covenant with Abraham centered on multiplication: "And he brought him outside and said, 'Look toward heaven, and number the stars, if you are able to number them.' Then he said to him, '*So shall your offspring be*'" (Genesis 15:5). This multiplication promise was powerfully restated after the test of Abraham's faith regarding the sacrifice of Isaac:

> By myself I have sworn, declares the Lord, because you have done this and have not withheld your son, your only son, I will surely bless you, and I will surely *multiply your offspring as the stars of heaven* and as the sand that is on the seashore. (Genesis 22:16-17)

When God made his covenant with Abraham, he made it clear that Abraham's offspring were also included in the promise.[4] In fact, since his promise was to multiply Abraham's descendants until they were as numerous as the stars in the sky and sand on the seashore, Abraham's descendants were by necessity incorporated into the promise.

ISAAC

The extension of the promise of multiplication is seen in God's restating and reaffirming the promise to Isaac, Abraham's son:

> I will *multiply your offspring as the stars of heaven* and will give to your offspring all these lands. And in your offspring all the nations of the earth shall be blessed, because Abraham obeyed my voice and kept my charge, my commandments, my statutes, and my laws. (Genesis 26:4-5)

JACOB

Likewise, God's promise was confirmed to Isaac's son Jacob:

> And behold, the Lord stood above it and said, "I am the Lord, the God of Abraham your father and the God of Isaac. The land on which you lie I will give to you and to your offspring. Your offspring *shall be like the dust of the earth*, and you shall spread abroad to the west and to the east and to the north and to the south, and in you and your offspring shall all the families of the earth be blessed. (Genesis 28:13-14)

MOSES

Moses led the descendants of Abraham, God's people, out of bondage in Egypt. At that time, Moses understood God's promises of multiplication to Abraham, Isaac, and Jacob to extend beyond those patriarchs. Moses even used it as the basis of his argument for why God should not wipe out Israel when God's wrath arose over them making the golden calf. Moses said to God:

> Remember Abraham, Isaac, and Israel, your servants, to whom you swore by your own self, and said to them, 'I will multiply your offspring as the stars of heaven, and all this land that I have promised I will give to your offspring, and they shall inherit it forever.' And the Lord relented from the disaster that he had spoken of bringing on his people. (Exodus 32:13-14)

DAVID

We see the enduring and extending nature of this promise as God repeats it many generations later to David and the Levitical priests:

> As the host of heaven cannot be numbered and the sands of the sea cannot be measured, so *I will multiply the offspring* of David my servant, and the Levitical priests who minister to me. (Jeremiah 33:22)

I love the words the Lord uses to illustrate multiplication—sand and stars. These are God's chosen word pictures demonstrating what he desires to do for his glory. Is it starting to become clear why I wanted you to get some sand between your toes and galaxies of stars in your gaze? Up to this point we have seen how God has given and reconfirmed his covenant promise of multiplication to the patriarchs and Levites. Be assured, though, that this promise is for *all* of Abraham's children who participate in the covenant through faith. He did it through them. He will do it through you.

ALL TRUE CHILDREN OF ABRAHAM

True children of Abraham are not those who descended from him physically, but those who have the same faith as he had. The apostle Paul is adamant about this. He says:

> Know then that it is *those of faith* who are the sons of Abraham. And the Scripture, foreseeing that God would justify the Gentiles by faith, preached the gospel beforehand to Abraham, saying, "In you shall all the nations be blessed." So then, *those who are of faith are blessed along with Abraham*, the man of faith. (Galatians 3:7-9)
>
> That is why it depends on faith, in order that the promise may rest on grace and be *guaranteed to all his offspring*—not only to the adherent of the law but also *to the one who shares the faith of Abraham, who is the father of us all.* (Romans 4:16)

Christ confirmed that the promise of a multiplying impact is offered to all with his parable of the soils:

> "But those that were sown on the good soil are the ones who hear the word and accept it and bear fruit, thirtyfold and sixtyfold and a hundredfold." (Mark 4:20)

These final verses illustrate that God's promise to make Abraham's descendants as numerous as the stars in the sky and the sand on the seashore are not only for Abraham, but also for all of us who share in his faith. This enduring promise is a foundation for us to trust God for the unbelievable, no matter how improbable it may seem.

IMPERATIVES IN THE NEW TESTAMENT

The doctrine of multiplication is also derived from the commands God gives his children in the New Testament. The Great Commission lays out plainly God's desire for his children to multiply disciples throughout the earth:[5]

> And Jesus came and said to them, "All authority in heaven and on earth has been given to me. Go therefore and make disciples of all nations, baptizing them in the name of the Father and of the Son and of the Holy Spirit, teaching them to observe all that I have commanded you. And behold, I am with you always, to the end of the age." (Matthew 28:18-20)

Jesus gave this command to his original disciples. Yet notice the command to make new disciples included teaching those disciples to obey all that Jesus had taught his original disciples. That would include this very same command to multiply.

The apostle Paul understood and passed along God's imperative to multiply to his young disciple Timothy. He said, "and what you have heard from me in the presence of many witnesses entrust to faithful men who will be able to teach others also" (2 Timothy 2:2).

EXAMPLES OF DISCIPLING IN THE SCRIPTURES

God's plan for multiplying laborers is illustrated in the mentoring relationships we see in the Bible. This mentoring took the form of on-the-job training, as mentors engaged with protégés and trained them to assist in the mentor's work.[6] A few notable examples of these relationships include the following:

- Moses and Joshua (Numbers 27:18-20)
- Elijah and Elisha (1 Kings 19:19-21)
- Jesus and the apostles (Mark 3:14-15)
- Barnabas and Paul (Acts 9:27; 11:22-26)
- Barnabas and John Mark (Acts 15:37-39)
- Paul and Timothy (2 Tim 2:2)

MISSION ACCOMPLISHED

We started in Genesis looking at God's plan to multiply a people for himself. Now we come to Revelation and see that mission completed:

> After this I looked, and behold, *a great multitude that no one could number, from every nation, from all tribes and peoples and languages*, standing before the throne and before the Lamb, clothed in white robes, with palm branches in their hands… (Revelation 7:9)

From cover to cover of the Bible, we see that God is going to accomplish his plan of spreading his glory throughout the earth by multiplying his people. He has no plan B. He needs no plan B. He will make his plan work.

OUR RESPONSE

Unfortunately, many have started on the journey toward spiritual multiplication only to abandon ship for some other approach to ministry when they hit headwinds or rough seas. But this cannot be our response if spiritual multiplication is the only plan God has given us. There are really only two things we can do if we are finding it difficult to raise up multiplying disciples.

The first is to re-examine our ministry practices and identify the ways in which we have deviated from the Master's model. The research presented in the rest of the book is an attempt to do just that. Hopefully, it will help you understand why some disciple-makers reproduce while others fail. Some of our findings will truly surprise and encourage you.

The second response is to do what Abraham did when it looked like his life would never multiply or bless the nations. In spite of all odds, he chose to trust God. He took him at his word and believed the Lord's promise to multiply his descendants to be as numerous as the stars in the sky and sand on the seashore. God wants to do that for you, too, as wild as that may seem. The next chapter is designed to unleash your faith to believe that God wants to use you and to help you gain an irresistible vision for your life.

Chapter 2

MAYBE SOMEONE ELSE

God might multiply his children through spiritual giants like Abraham or Elijah or Billy Graham, but it is hard to believe that he would do it through me." Do your weaknesses and inexperience make it seem impossible that your spiritual descendants would one day be too numerous to count? If you're like me, you probably think, "Maybe God will do it through someone else, but not me."

The Holy Spirit knew that Satan would try to get us to believe a lie like that, so he inspired James to address the issue.

> Elijah was a man *with a nature like ours*, and he prayed fervently that it might not rain, and for three years and six months it did not rain on the earth. Then he prayed again, and heaven gave rain, and the earth bore its fruit. (James 5:17-18)

God didn't answer Elijah's prayers because he was a "spiritual giant." In fact, James says he was just like you and me—warts, fears, disbeliefs, and all. You might be thinking, "But James says in the prior verse (5:16) that God answers the prayer of a 'righteous person,' and I don't feel very righteous." Exactly! This is the reason the Spirit pointed out we are no different from Elijah. God answers the prayer of the righteous. Elijah was righteous and he had a nature just like you and me. Sinful. He needed to get his righteousness just like you and I get ours—through Christ. Even the apostle Paul confessed his righteousness was not his own:

> ...and be found in him, not having a righteousness of my own that comes from the law, but that which comes through faith in Christ, the righteousness from God that depends on faith... (Philippians 3:9)

Don't disqualify yourself in your mind from a work for which Jesus died to qualify you. How greatly God multiplies his children through you depends more on who *he* is than on who *you* are. Let's look at this God who promised to multiply your descendants.

THE GOD OF STARS AND SAND

In 1 Corinthians 3:9 we read, "For we are God's fellow workers." Understand this is not an equal partnership. Our part of the work is important. The crops won't come up if the farmer doesn't put seed in the ground. But it is God who does the miraculous part of the work, making them actually grow. He does the heavy lifting of multiplying our efforts. The question is not how qualified *you* are to multiply spiritually. The real question is, how qualified is *God* to keep his promise? Is he capable of multiplying your descendants until they are as numerous as the stars in the sky and sand on the seashore?

The heavens give us insight into God's nature and power. The Psalmist says,

> The heavens declare the glory of God;
> the skies proclaim the work of his hands.
> Day after day they pour forth speech;
> night after night they display knowledge. (Psalm 19:1-2)

We should stop and contemplate what type of power must have been behind the creation of the universe. The heavens are, after all, continually pouring forth certain truths about God and his glory.

There is a star named Betelgeuse that is 527 light years from Earth. If we translate that number into miles, it is (read this number out loud to get a greater sense of its enormity) three quadrillion, ninety-seven trillion, nine hundred sixty-nine billion, four hundred two million, seventy-six thousand, two hundred eighty-five miles. Whose creative energy produced a star so far away from Earth? Wonderfully, it is the same God who promises to multiply your life according to his power. Now for the punch line. The astonishing thing about Betelgeuse is not its distance from the Earth. Compared to the farthest visible stars, which we have found with the Hubble telescope, Betelgeuse is really close to the Earth. Astronomers estimate that the farthest stars they have detected are between thirteen and fifteen billion light years from Earth. When you compare Betelgeuse's distance of 527 light years to fifteen billion, it seems like you can reach out and touch it!

The thing that boggles my mind, though, is not Betelgeuse's distance from Earth, but its size. Before I tell you its size, let me first tell you that the Earth's orbit around the sun is 583 million miles. Betelgeuse's size? Twice the size of the Earth's orbit around the sun. What kind of creative power created a single object that large? The same kind that is committed to multiplying your life!

Betelgeuse is just one star, though. Let's zoom our focus out and look at the larger universe. Our Milky Way has somewhere between 200 and 400 billion stars. Considering that each of those 200 billion stars averages a distance of 29 trillion miles from another star, our galaxy is a pretty big place, to say the least. Furthermore, our galaxy, as bewilderingly vast as it is, is only one of 200 billion or more galaxies in the universe.

Before I went on my first summer mission trip, our team leader required everyone who was going to memorize a specific passage of Scripture. As you will see below, it was no easy task. Most people just memorize the last three verses of this passage. They are the verses where the Lord promises to give strength to the weary. Our drill-sergeant team leader made us memorize the entire passage. Why? Because the certainty of a promise depends on the ability of its giver to deliver on what was promised. The verses before the promise in this passage demonstrate that its giver can certainly make good on his pledge. To get the most out of reading this passage, may I remind you that you are sitting on a beach under the starry host? And if you really want to experience the encouragement from this passage that the Lord intended, read it aloud and with gusto. Doing so will make the reading ten times better.

> Do you not know?
>   Have you not heard?
> Has it not been told you from the beginning?
>   Have you not understood since the earth was founded?
> He sits enthroned above the circle of the earth,
>   and its people are like grasshoppers.

He stretches out the heavens like a canopy,
    and spreads them out like a tent to live in.
He brings princes to naught
    and reduces the rulers of this world to nothing.
No sooner are they planted,
    no sooner are they sown,
    no sooner do they take root in the ground,
than he blows on them and they wither,
    and a whirlwind sweeps them away like chaff.
"To whom will you compare me?
    Or who is my equal?" says the Holy One.
Lift your eyes and look to the heavens:
    Who created all these?
He who brings out the starry host one by one,
    and calls them each by name.
Because of his great power and mighty strength,
    not one of them is missing.
Why do you say, O Jacob,
    and complain, O Israel,
"My way is hidden from the LORD;
    my cause is disregarded by my God"?
Do you not know?
    Have you not heard?
The LORD is the everlasting God,
    the Creator of the ends of the earth.
He will not grow tired or weary,
    and his understanding no one can fathom.
He gives strength to the weary
    and increases the power of the weak.
Even youths grow tired and weary,
    and young men stumble and fall;
but those who hope in the LORD
    will renew their strength.
They will soar on wings like eagles;
    they will run and not grow weary,
    they will walk and not be faint. (Isaiah 40:21-31)

GOD'S POWER AND FAITHFULNESS ILLUSTRATED

How greatly God multiplies his children through you depends more on who *he* is than who you are. He can take even our most feeble efforts and do more with them than we ever imagined. This is clearly seen in the lives of Swedish missionaries David and Svea Flood.[7]

In 1921, the young couple, along with their two-year-old son David, moved to Congo, which is in the heart of Africa. They teamed up with another Scandinavian couple, Joel and Bertha Erickson. After months of laboring in a remote part of the jungle, Joel reached his limit and angrily vented to David, "This is ridiculous!"

"What is ridiculous?" David asked.

"Everything! Coming to this God-forsaken continent. Traipsing through the jungles. Living like animals. Nearly killing our wives. And you've got little David who'll probably die of malaria."[8] Joel went on to ask, "What do we have to show for months of work? Malaria, malnutrition, two village chiefs furious with us—"

"There's a native boy," David answered quietly.

"Yes, the boy!" Joel replied. "Our one convert! For all these months, we have one conversion to report—a child, who probably doesn't understand a thing we say. I'm sorry David. We have to go."[9]

Though the Ericksons left, the Floods stayed on alone. To complicate things further, Svea became pregnant and gave birth to a little girl. They named her Aina, a classical Swedish name. However, the birth process and complications from malaria were too much for Svea. The Lord took her home when Aina was just seventeen days old.

David dug a crude grave for his beloved wife. As he stood over it, he thought, "What a wasted life." Something in him snapped, and he was filled with anger and bitterness toward God. He felt he had been sent on a fool's mission. He had had enough. David took his two motherless children and headed to the missionary outpost where the Ericksons had gone. When they finally arrived at the outpost, the Ericksons urged David not to take Aina on the grueling journey to the nearest port. It was a nightmare of a trip, and little Aina would certainly not survive it. Determined to return to Sweden and start his life over again, David reluctantly agreed. So he left his infant daughter with the Ericksons as he and little David headed back to Sweden.

Within eight months, both of the Ericksons died suddenly, so nine-month-old Aina was given to American missionaries Arthur and Anna Berg. They changed her name slightly to Agnes, and her friends called her Aggie. When she was three, the family moved back to the States where Aggie grew up.

Aggie married and had children of her own. She and her husband Dewey were given a vacation to Sweden for their twenty-fifth wedding anniversary. Aggie would finally have a chance to meet the father who had left her in Africa. When she met him, he was living in a little apartment building in a lower-class section of Stockholm. Her father's room was squalid and had dust-covered empty liquor bottles lining every windowsill. Diabetes and a stroke had confined this seventy-three-year-old man to his apartment for three years. As Aggie looked into the far corner of the room, she saw his small wrinkled frame, his sunken cheeks which needed a shave, and his short, unkempt head of white hair.

Her half-brother Bengt touched their father and said, "Papa, Aina's here." He turned toward her slowly. She took his hand and said, "Papa?"

He began to weep, saying, "I never meant to give you away."

After crying with him for a while, she said, "It's all right Papa," and took him in her arms and held him like a baby. "God took care of me," she said.

He stiffened suddenly and the tears stopped. "God forgot all of us," he spat angrily. "Our lives have been like this because of him. I was in Africa all that time, and only one little boy … And then your mother …"

As she wiped tobacco stains from his chin, she said, "Papa, I've got a story to tell you, and it is a true one. You didn't go to Africa in vain. Mama didn't die in vain. The little boy you won to the Lord grew up to win that whole village to Christ. The little seed you planted just kept growing and growing. Today, there are six hundred African people serving the Lord because you were faithful to the call of God in your life."

A few years later, Aggie attended a high-level evangelism conference in London, England, where a report was given from the nation of Zaire (the former Belgian Congo). The superintendent of the national church, representing some 110,000 baptized believers, spoke eloquently of the gospel's spread in his nation. Afterward Aggie asked him if he had ever heard of

David and Svea Flood. "Yes, madam," the man replied, "It was Svea Flood who led me to Jesus Christ."

Aggie said, "I am their daughter. I was born on that mountaintop." Suddenly, tears ran down the man's face, and he said, "Thank you for letting your mother die so that we can live."

After this, Aggie had the chance to travel to Zaire to visit her mother's grave and worship with the believers there. In the worship service that day, the pastor read the Scripture, "Truly, truly, I say to you, unless a grain of wheat falls into the earth and dies, it remains alone; but if it dies, it bears much fruit" (John 12:24). Svea had given her life that others might live.

"THROUGH US" VERSUS "WITH US"

We must understand what God may choose to do through us is often much greater than what God does with us. What did God do with David and Svea Flood? Together they led one boy to Christ. But as we have seen, what God did through them was much, much more. That's the beauty of spiritual multiplication.

There is another example of this much closer to home for me. In the early 1980s on the campus of the University of North Alabama, a young lady named Sandra began meeting with a younger girl named Tammy. Her goal was to help her grow spiritually and learn to multiply her life. Before long a new believer named Susan saw the growth in Tammy's life. She asked Tammy to start meeting with her to help her grow in Christ and prepare to multiply, like Sandra was helping Tammy. The next year Susan went away to graduate school where she met a young campus minister. Me. I was busy evangelizing and discipling men with the dream of raising up a team to go to the unreached. We fell in love and married. A year and a half later we moved to Bangkok with our long-term team of three couples and five singles. After learning to speak Thai, Susan developed relationships with Thai women. One of the women that came to Christ was named Git. After being discipled by Susan for a while, Git in turn led another woman to Christ named Bui. Bui turned out to be quite the evangelist and led many others to Christ. Some of them are Snow, Gift, Pook, Gob, Joy, Gookgui, Fone, Kol, and Mam. Several of these women have gone on to lead others to Christ.

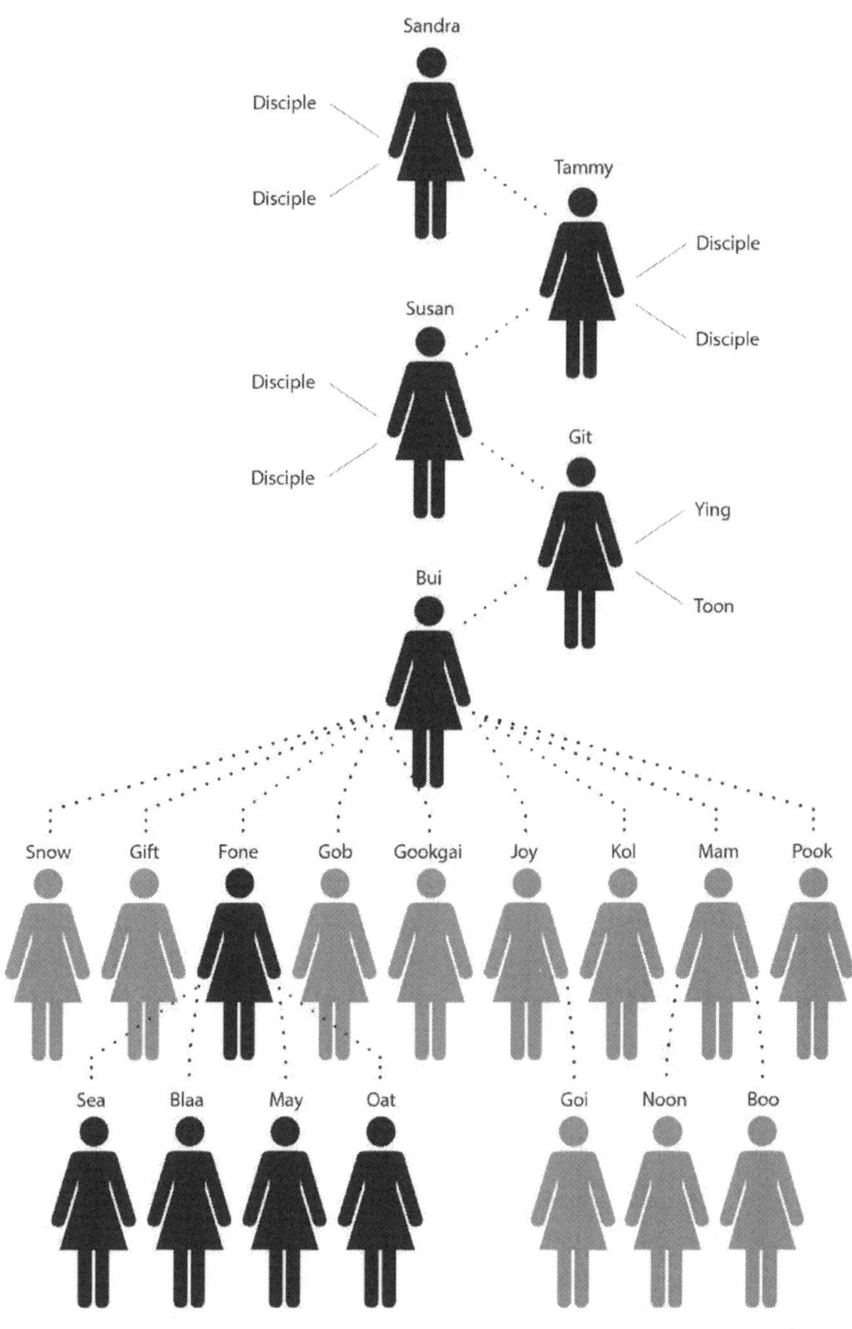
Sandra
Disciple
Disciple
Tammy
Disciple
Disciple
Susan
Disciple
Disciple
Git
Ying
Toon
Bui
Snow
Gift
Fone
Gob
Gookgai
Joy
Kol
Mam
Pook
Sea
Blaa
May
Oat
Goi
Noon
Boo

Take Fone for example. She led Oat, May, Blaa, and Sea to Christ. This chain of multiplication endures to this day and continues to grow and expand exponentially. The graphic to the left pictures just some of the multiplication that has taken place.

God is able! I watched this story unfold, and I know the players well. Git lived in our house while Susan discipled her, and Bui babysat my daughters. None of them are spiritual superstars. They are ordinary people who have chosen to trust God and give their lives away. I have personally witnessed the *edifying* power of a discipling relationship. But I have also seen the *enduring* nature of this type of ministry and the *explosive* growth potential it has for the kingdom of Christ. Who did this story start with? Sandra. She never moved out of the Southeast United States. Yet she has impacted people on the other side of the planet who had never heard the gospel. Susan left Thailand after ten years, yet her ministry impact there continues to grow and multiply to this day. Git hasn't preached to the masses or led dozens of women to Christ, but she was faithful to win and disciple a few, and God continues to expand her impact.

Jesus discipled twelve men. He trained them to reproduce. What would happen if you decided to do the same? Let's look at what would happen in twelve years if your goal was to just win one person to Christ per year and train them to do the same. At the end of the first year, there would be two of you seeking to multiply. If you both led someone to Christ the next year, there would be four of you. After three years, there would be eight. Not huge, but stay with me. After six years, there would be sixty-four, and after twelve years there would be 4,096 of you. That's growth. You would have personally only discipled twelve people, but you would have impacted thousands! God can do much more through you than he actually does with you.

While we lived in Thailand, we had the privilege of having Jim Downing, former Deputy President of the Navigators, come for a visit. While eating breakfast one morning, I asked him the following question: "Jim, you had the opportunity to work with Billy Graham from the early days. You watched his ministry develop over the years. Why do you think Billy's ministry grew so dramatically while other evangelists' ministries of that time didn't?" Jim's answer was simple. "Billy had the faith to go rent the stadium when others didn't." I was speechless and challenged to trust God for more.

The spiritual principle is true. "You do not have because you do not ask" (James 4:2). What are you asking God to do with your life? If it's not intimidating to you, it probably is insulting to God.

Is it crazy to ask God to multiply your life exponentially? If your trust is in yourself, yes. If your trust is in God who created the stars and sand, no. Remember how God encouraged Abraham to understand and believe this promise.

"And he brought him outside and said, 'Look toward heaven, and number the stars, if you are able to number them.' Then he said to him, '*So shall your offspring be*'" (Genesis 15:5). Thankfully, Abraham gazed at the stars and believed God for what seemed impossible. Will you? It's a prerequisite for spiritual multiplication in the real world.

CHAPTER 3

TROUBLE IN MULTIPLICATION PARADISE

I came to Christ as a senior in high school. The next year, when I went to college, I had the opportunity to go on a Christian retreat for entering freshmen. Hungry to grow spiritually, I jumped at the chance. At the retreat, some of each student's time was spent in small group discussions led by upperclassmen. My small group leader was a pre-med student named Jay. He had a mature walk with the Lord that had been developed over many years. He had been discipled by a campus minister the previous year and was now ready to start discipling others.

During the retreat, Jay saw my desire to grow spiritually and to make an impact for Christ. So, a week after classes began, he invited me to lunch in the cafeteria to challenge me into a "Discipleship Group" he was starting. I had barely begun to eat when Jay launched into explaining how Jesus had set an example for us regarding how to go about ministry. He explained while Jesus loved the world and helped many, his primary focus was on his twelve disciples. More than that, there were three disciples, Peter, James and John, who formed sort of an inner circle with whom Jesus spent even more time.

Before long, Jay started diagramming 2 Timothy 2:2 ("and what you have heard from me in the presence of many witnesses entrust to faithful men who will be able to teach others also.") on a napkin. It looked something like the diagram on the next page.

He explained how Paul had followed Jesus' example in disciple-making and that we were to do the same.

Then he turned the napkin over, redrew the diagram, and wrote my name on the second level. He then drew other levels below me. I could

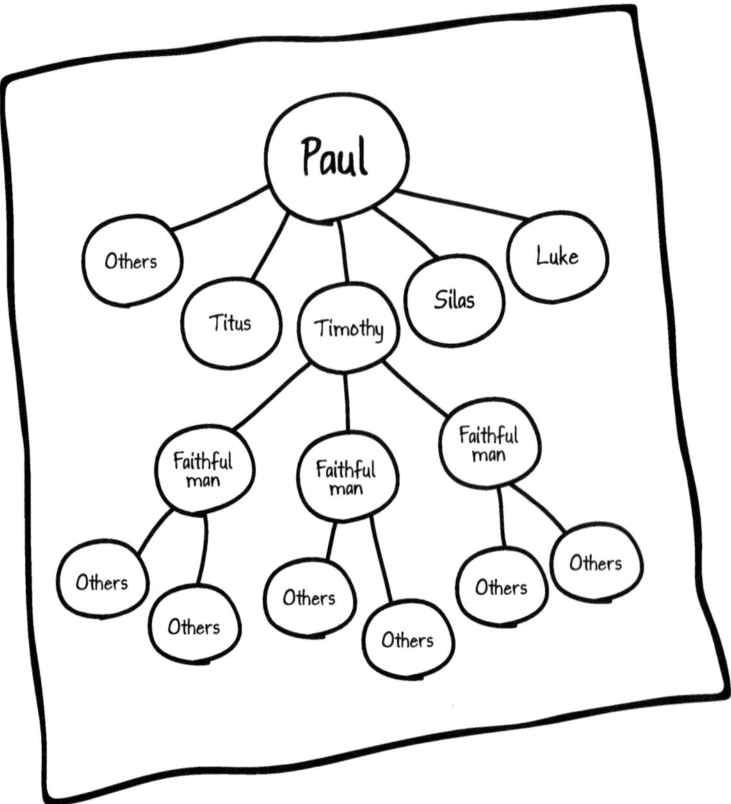

see how after I had been discipled for a year, I could begin to disciple others. They would in turn disciple still others, and so on. My excitement grew as I saw I could leave behind sixty-four multiplying disciples when I graduated. Jay then went on to explain how my great, great grandchildren in the Lord could carry on the work of making disciples on the campus long after I was gone. As Jay explained the vision of spiritual multiplication, the lights came on. I was all in. Jesus' ministry strategy suddenly made perfect sense. The command to "Go and make disciples" (Matthew 28:18-20) was instantly clarified. I would no longer read it as merely a command to tell others about Christ. It was more than that. The goal was not proclamation, but reproduction—disciples who multiply other disciples.

In the coming weeks, I began noticing more and more verses in the Bible confirming the idea. I had been called to the adventure of following Jesus in multiplying spiritually. The meaning of John 20:21, "As the Father has sent me, I am sending you," was so clear now. I started claiming promises of spiritual multiplication like Mark 4:20, "Others, like seed sown on good soil, hear the word, accept it, and produce a crop—thirty, sixty, or even a hundred times what was sown"(NIV).

During my freshman year, Jay poured his life into me and three other students. He would often stop by my dorm room and ask me if I wanted to have a quiet time together. A visit for an extended time of prayer was not unusual. There were times when Jay took me out to train me in sharing my faith. We went to the local putt-putt golf course, a game room where high school students hung out, and a local mall. Other times, his focus was on character building. Once he even sat me down and gently rebuked me for a prideful attitude he had noticed in me. It was a tremendous year of growth.

When the next school year began, I challenged four freshmen in my fraternity to enter into the disciple-making process with me. The group started meeting with great excitement. By the end of the year, though, only one of my disciples continued to meet with me. But I didn't throw in the towel and give up on multiplying disciples. I was determined to learn from my failures. I prayerfully sought out and challenged other young men into the process of spiritual multiplication. Over the next couple of years, by God's grace, I saw fruit in both my evangelism efforts and in my attempts to equip men to multiply. I saw from my own experience and that of other student disciple-makers that, while the road to multiplying was sometimes bumpy and frustrating, it was a journey worth taking. My belief was confirmed: the vision of spiritual multiplication could become a reality.

Because I believe multiplying disciples is the best way to see the world reached for Christ, I joined the staff of a campus ministry built on that philosophy of ministry. The ministry had a clear vision statement: to help university students become laborers for Christ on campus and then to send them out into the lost world to multiply for a lifetime. I poured my heart and soul into seeing this vision become a reality. God was faithful and honored my efforts with direct fruit and fruit through the students I led. Once again, my confidence in the vision of spiritual multiplication was fortified.

THE FIRST SIGNS OF TROUBLE

After I had been on staff with the campus ministry for a couple of years, I started to notice something. The men I had discipled previously, who were now out in the real world, were struggling in personal ministry. They were not experiencing anything like the level of fruitfulness they had when they were students. There was one graduate from another campus who was doing well. He had joined the Air Force and gotten involved with a disciple-making ministry called The Navigators. He was seeing fruit in his personal ministry. Interestingly, I kept seeing this one graduate's success story told over and over in different campus ministry staff's newsletters. I began to wonder why I wasn't seeing other graduates' stories told. I started to realize that it wasn't just the men I had previously discipled who were failing to be fruitful in the workplace. Other campus ministry staff's disciples were also having difficulty multiplying after graduation. The seriousness of this problem was not lost on me. I was deeply disturbed by the implications of this problem. The validity of our vision to train students on the campus to go reproduce disciples in the real world was called into question. More than that, the whole dream of seeing the world reached for Christ at an exponentially growing rate was in jeopardy. I didn't want to merely help students be fruitful for the four years they were on the university campus. I longed to see them go and make disciples for the next *forty* years after they graduated. Our research and this book grew out of this burden.

THE QUEST FOR AN ANSWER BEGINS

While this book certainly is not the last word on the subject, it is my humble attempt to outline some of our major findings about what it takes to successfully multiply disciples in the real world. When this problem first came to my attention during my mid-twenties, my method for coming up with solutions to it wasn't very scientific. As I discovered later through years of real life experience and quantitative research, the conclusions I drew then were often wrong. What method did I use? It is embarrassing to admit, but my *modus operandi* was basically this: I would spend time visiting with a graduate from our campus ministry and ask questions about his or her life. Anything that didn't seem to make common (ministry) sense was labeled as the culprit. What is worse, these conclusions quickly showed up in talks that were given to graduating seniors on what it would take for them to be successful in the real world. And now, years later, I'm still hearing people share faulty information about what it takes to successfully multiply in the workplace.

EARLY THEORIES

Here are some examples of my first conclusions and how I came to them.

1. THE "POOR JOB AND LIVING SITUATION CHOICES" THEORY

One of the young men whom I discipled graduated and got a good job working for a well-known publishing company. Though he had a heart for the lost, he was not seeing people come to Christ. As I began to probe, I found out he was rarely sharing the gospel. When I asked why he wasn't sharing at work, he explained that he worked in a department of the company that was staffed entirely by women except for him. He felt it wasn't appropriate to make a group of women the focus of his evangelistic efforts.

Around the same time, I talked with another graduate. He had landed a job as a traveling salesman for an appliance company. Much of his day was spent driving from store to store. He had little prolonged contact with people throughout the day. To make things worse, to save money he and his young bride rented a house from his father that was located in a neighborhood full of people in their fifties and sixties. It seemed apparent to me why these men were not seeing their lives yield the same level of fruit that they had as students. They lacked extended and meaningful daily contact with lost people their own age and gender. They needed to select a job and living situation that daily immersed them in significant contact with lost people like them. It all seemed perfectly logical to me. There is no impact without contact, right? Actually, our research showed that there are other factors far more important than where you live or with whom you work. In fact, we found no statistically significant relationship between where one lives and effectiveness in disciple-making, nor between the number of lost people with whom one works closely on a daily basis. Hard to believe, but true.

2. THE "IT JUST TAKES A FEW YEARS AFTER GRADUATION TO ADJUST" THEORY

Another popular theory I heard floating around for a while was, after one graduates, there is a period of adjustment that impacts ministry fruitfulness negatively. Then, after one gets used to his or her new life circumstances, ministry fruitfulness will increase. Unfortunately, time has proven this theory to be more of a myth than a reality.

3. THE "INSUFFICIENT PREPARATION" THEORY

As the campus ministry I was a part of and others like it wrestled with this problem, our solutions inevitably involved improving our training or adding to it. We started by offering graduating seniors a one-hour workshop at our conferences. Over time, the one-hour workshop grew into weekend conferences on the subject of multiplication after graduation. We developed training notebooks and added career testing and counseling. To be honest, nothing helped much. Finally, I concluded and our research confirmed that the problem was not with our training. No amount of improvement in our training would help. Improving a solution is to no avail if it is the wrong answer to the problem. If someone has a broken arm, they don't need a better antibiotic. They need it straightened and put in a cast. Most ministries I know of provide excellent training. The failure of graduates to multiply in the real world is not a result of deficiencies in their instruction. The problem lies elsewhere.

4. THE "IT'S JUST TOO HARD IN THE REAL WORLD" THEORY

This theory is also not true. After wondering for several years if spiritual multiplication in the real world was even possible, I began to meet individuals who were, in fact, seeing God multiply their lives in the workplace. Some were in their thirties and had kids. Others were empty-nesters. Some had the gift of evangelism. Most didn't. They were ordinary people, dealing with the same struggles we all do. Yet they were multiplying. They lived in Asia, South America, Africa, and even in the United States. Thankfully, they proved for us that spiritual multiplication in the real world is in fact possible. Seeing their fruit spurred me on to find out what set them apart from other people. Why did they succeed at multiplying when others failed?

THE BIBLE, RESEARCH, OR BOTH?

The Bible is our infallible guide for life and ministry. The book in your hand is first and foremost based on biblical principles of ministry. We will study these principles in the model of Christ, the master disciple-maker. Besides the Bible, God also makes himself and his ways known through general revelation. In Romans it says, "For his invisible attributes, namely, his eternal power and divine nature, have been clearly perceived, ever since the creation of the world, in the things that have been made" (Romans 1:20). Learning things through general revelation in addition to special revelation (the Bible) is not bad. God wants us to learn from both. There are certain things we learn from general revelation through the scientific process of discovery we would never learn from reading the Scriptures, and vice-versa. For example, we learn through experimentation, not the Bible, that if we mix red and blue we get purple. On the other hand, experimentation doesn't tell us about who created color in the first place. Nor how we relate to him. I believe the things we learn through general revelation about ministry must be filtered through the grid of biblical principles. We should interpret our research findings in light of Scripture, not vice versa. Research, however, can play a valuable role in helping us learn how to appropriately *apply* biblical principles.

PRINCIPLES AND APPLICATIONS

Biblical principles of ministry are not that complicated or hard to understand. Most young Christians can understand them the first time the principles are taught. The hard thing is understanding how to actually apply the principles.

I'm reminded of what Dwight Eisenhower said about the principles of war:

> The basic principles of strategy are so simple that a child may understand them. But to determine their proper application to a given situation requires the hardest kind of work . . .[10]

When it comes to determining proper applications of biblical principles of ministry, we sometimes have difficulty because some principles seem to contradict each other. On my bookshelf right now I have a book by one author who is espousing friendship evangelism as the most biblical approach. On the same shelf, you will find another which takes great pains to show that proclamation evangelism, not friendship evangelism, is the proper approach. Which is right? Are both the need to proclaim the gospel and the need to befriend sinners taught in Scripture? Yes. The problem is the Bible never tells us exactly when in the process of developing the friendship we should proclaim the gospel. We have some examples in Scripture of how people went about evangelism, but those should be taken as descriptive of what happened and not prescriptive of how we should always do evangelism. Good research can help us learn how to best apply biblical principles to our various contexts.

Our survey research was conducted for that very reason. We sought to discover answers to questions like these:

1. Who led more people to Christ over a three-year period?
    a. People who shared the gospel within the first few times they interacted with someone
    b. People who waited until they had an established friendship
    c. People who varied their approach
2. Would having twelve months of evangelism training help you lead more people to Christ than just taking a weekend seminar on the subject?
3. Does the number of children you have affect your effectiveness in spiritual multiplication?
4. Does the number of lost people your job puts you into contact with on a regular basis influence your effectiveness in disciple-making?
5. When discipling others, what is best to do?
    a. Stick with a core set of materials
    b. Use different materials according to the needs of the individual or group
    c. Use a core set of materials and add additional materials as needed
    d. Don't use any materials
6. Is there a common set of characteristics that can be found in the churches attended by highly effective disciple-makers? If so, what are they?

7. What should you do in your small group meeting to help your disciples multiply?

The findings related to these questions, and many more discussed later, may surprise you. More than that, though, the answers will increase your effectiveness in disciple-making. The results of our study are encouraging. They show that ordinary Christians can multiply spiritually in the real world. They also delineate the types of environments and behaviors that are required for success. This is not at all intended to create a formulaic approach to disciple-making or to diminish the role of the Holy Spirit. It is, however, meant to remind us there are laws of the harvest that have been established by the Lord. We will highlight some of those laws which are critical if we want to see the harvest multiplied. God will be faithful to do his part to multiply our lives, but that does not mean that the work on our side of the equation is not important. How well we labor will affect the fruitfulness of our ministries. We cannot carelessly throw seed on rocks and expect God to work against the principles of growth he has established. To be honest, stories of failed attempts at spiritual multiplication are more common than success stories. It doesn't have to be that way. Thoughtful application of biblical principles can yield explosive results!

QUESTIONS ABOUT RESEARCH CONDUCTED

What type of research was done?

We did both quantitative (a web-based survey with closed-ended questions) and qualitative (face-to-face interviews with open-ended questions).

How many people were included in the web-based survey?

410

What factors determined if someone was considered highly effective, effective, or non-effective in disciple-making?

1. How many people they led to Christ in the previous three years
2. How many people their disciples led to Christ in the previous three years

3. How many spiritual generations have been produced through their discipling efforts

What thresholds were used to determine levels of effectiveness?

Thresholds	Minimum number of people they must have led to Christ in the past three years	Minimum number of their disciples who must have led someone to Christ in the past three years	Minimum number of spiritual generations below them
Highly Effective	2	2	3
Effective	1	1	2
Non-Effective	0	0	1

Isn't the threshold to be considered highly effective pretty low?

Only 12 percent of the people surveyed were found to be highly effective. These disciple-makers truly stand out in the crowd. Studying the differences between them and the rest proved extremely helpful. You may be interested to know that 33 percent of those surveyed were found to be "effective" and the remaining 55 percent were "non-effective."

What types of questions did the survey contain?

The survey asked sixty-five questions. Over forty questions were aimed at discovering differences between non-effective, effective, and highly effective disciple-makers in the following areas:[11]

- Personal life demographics (location, age, marital status, gender, number of children, working environment, etc.)
- Characteristics of their church or para-church ministry (age, size, leadership, vision, training, approach to ministry, evangelism practices, prayer habits, etc.)

- The type, source, and extent of training they received (evangelism training, discipling, coaching, etc.)
- Their personal approach to ministry (evangelism, use of materials, small group activities, prayer, etc.)

Where did the people you surveyed live?

Initially, we just studied the responses from people who lived in the southeastern United States. Then, we analyzed the responses received from those who lived in the rest of the world. Interestingly, there was no statistically significant difference in the findings between the two groups. This similarity gives us confidence that what we will be sharing with you are truly transcultural principles of ministry and can be applied anywhere.

Were the highly effective disciple-makers "Super Christians"?

No. If we had found no consistent contextual or behavioral factors in this group, we would just have to consider them super Christians or flukes. Thankfully, that was not the case. We now know about the environments they live in and how they go about ministry. We can learn from them and become highly effective too.

What would happen through my life if I did what these highly effective disciple-makers did?

We have calculated that if a twenty-two-year-old will make disciples at the same modest rate our highly effective disciple-makers have proved possible (as shown on the previous page), they will impact 22,619,537 people by the time they are seventy-eight. Wow! Many of the people we surveyed exceeded the minimum thresholds needed to be considered highly effective. Even if you only experienced half of the level of effectiveness in multiplying as our calculations assume, you will still have impacted millions of people in your lifetime. Millions of people would be hard to count, so perhaps an easier way of expressing how God used your life would be to say "he multiplied your spiritual descendants so that they are as numerous as the stars in the sky and sand in the seashore." Since we have seen that spiritual multiplication in the real world is in fact possible, let's move on now to discovering the factors that are necessary to see this vision become a reality.

Part 2

Effective Disciple-Making Contexts

Chapter 4

SOIL

When we lived in Thailand, some friends of ours gave us a small banana tree. They came over to the house and helped us plant it in our back yard. We were excited about the idea that one day we would be able to just step into our backyard and pick part of our morning breakfast. Unfortunately, not long after that, our landlord decided to sell the house we were renting. After finding a new house and moving all of our furniture, I went back to our old house, shovel in hand. I wanted bananas from that tree! I carefully dug it up and moved it to our new house. As the weeks went by, though, the little tree just didn't seem to grow. I began to wonder if the move was just too hard on it or if the tree was somehow defective. My vision of eating bananas from my own tree in the tropics began to fade. Then the thought occurred to me, "Maybe the problem is not with the tree. Maybe the problem is with the soil." I devised a simple plan. Each evening I would pick up our Golden Retriever's droppings from the yard. I put them under the tree and watered it well. Problem solved! The little tree began to grow at a noticeable rate and started bearing fruit. Finally, the vision had become a reality!

There is an idea out there that the college campus is the perfect environment to make disciples but that it is somehow not the real world. The idea is that when a disciple has trouble multiplying after graduation, it is because the workplace is just a tougher environment. As we have seen previously, though, this myth has thankfully been debunked. There are highly effective disciple-makers who multiply in all kinds of situations. So if the real world context is not the problem, what is? Let's consider the transplanted banana tree illustration a little more carefully. A fruit tree actually lives in two environments, one above ground and one below. The above ground environment is where the tree bears fruit (college campus or real world). The below ground environment is where the tree gets a lot of what it needs to bear fruit (campus ministry or local church). My banana tree wasn't having difficulty bearing fruit because the above ground environment was too harsh. No, the problem was that it wasn't getting the nutrients it needed from the soil in which it was planted.

Could it be that simple? Could successful college disciple-makers struggle after graduation, not because it's harder "out there," but because the new soil isn't providing them with what they need to bear fruit? Let's think about it for a minute. When they walked across the stage and were handed their diplomas, they didn't suddenly lose all of the training they had received. The DNA that was in them, the vision and conviction to multiply, remains. Maybe there is nothing wrong with the tree. Maybe the problem is with the new context into which their roots get transplanted. College disciple-making movements provide the nutrients of leadership, vision, encouragement, fellowship, teamwork, accountability, and coaching needed to bear fruit in personal ministry.[12] Unfortunately, most graduates are transplanted into churches that don't function as disciple-making movements. They fail to provide their members with what they need to continue bearing fruit. Thankfully, our research revealed a number of churches who are doing a great job of helping their members function as disciple-making teams. We need to learn from these churches.

In Mark 4, Jesus uses a parable about seed that was sown into four different soils. In each case, the seed was good. The difference in fruitfulness was not the seed, but rather the context in which the seed was planted. In the parable, the teaching emphasis was on the need for a receptive and obedient heart. Still, the physical principle Jesus mentioned—about a seed needing good soil to grow—holds true in our context. As we will discuss further, a believer placed in the environment of a healthy local church that functions as a disciple-making movement has a far greater chance of multiplying his or her life than one who isn't. Let me put it bluntly. You can't put healthy laborers into an unhealthy church and expect them to successfully multiply their lives. It just won't happen.

AN ARMY OF ONE

From 2001 to 2006, the United States Army used the recruiting slogan "An Army of One." The five-year life span for this slogan was short compared to the "Be All You Can Be" slogan that preceded it. It lasted for twenty-one years. The slogan "An Army of One" received a lot of criticism because it suggested individualism. This went against the Army's value of teamwork. Many suspect this is the reason why the slogan was pulled. The Army values teamwork because it knows that teams, not individuals, win wars. Without the support of the rest of the team, no individual soldier will last long in battle or make much of an impact on the enemy.

Individual laborers are not miniature bodies of Christ. When we study spiritual gifts, we quickly recognize that no believer has all of the gifts, and because of this, we need each other. However, when it comes to disciple-making, somehow we tend to think that individuals can go out and do it on their own. This is a root cause of why so many fail to reproduce.

God exists in a constant state of community. The Father and the Son and the Holy Spirit enjoy an eternal oneness and fellowship. God also designed us to live in community with him and with the rest of the body of Christ. Fish don't do well outside of water because they weren't designed to live that way. Laborers don't do well outside of disciple-making movements because they weren't designed to live and function that way.

WHY WE NEED EACH OTHER

From the time of creation, we were designed to live in community. Additionally, the fall's corruption of the flesh created another reason we need each other. Our now weakened flesh often has difficulty carrying out the healthy desires of our spirit. Jesus pointed to this reality when he found his disciples unable to pray for even an hour without falling asleep. "The spirit indeed is willing, but the flesh is weak" (Matthew 26:41). Unfortunately, I know this truth all too well. I have set plenty of goals in my life, concerning just about everything you can imagine, only to discover that "the spirit indeed is willing, but the flesh is weak." What about you? Have you made New Year's resolutions regarding exercise, prayer, diets, or Bible reading and then failed? Of course. We all have. "The spirit indeed is willing, but the flesh is weak."

God offers us a way to have victory over the flesh. We see the answer in Hebrews:

> And let us consider and give attentive, continuous care to watching over one another, studying how we may stir up (stimulate and incite) to

> love and helpful deeds and noble activities, not forsaking or neglecting to assemble together [as believers], as is the habit of some people, but admonishing (warning, urging, and encouraging) one another, and all the more faithfully as you see the day approaching. (Hebrews 10:24-25, Amplified Bible)

If we didn't need others to spur us on to love and good deeds, God wouldn't tell us to do that. We can have all the training and good intentions in the world regarding evangelism and disciple-making, but if we are not in a community that spurs us on, we will fail. Let me illustrate from our research.

We asked the participants in our survey how much evangelism training they had received. We also asked them how many people they had led to Christ in the three year period prior to taking the survey. Conventional wisdom would lead one to believe that those who had received more training would have led more people to Christ. If that were the case, the results on a graph might look like this.

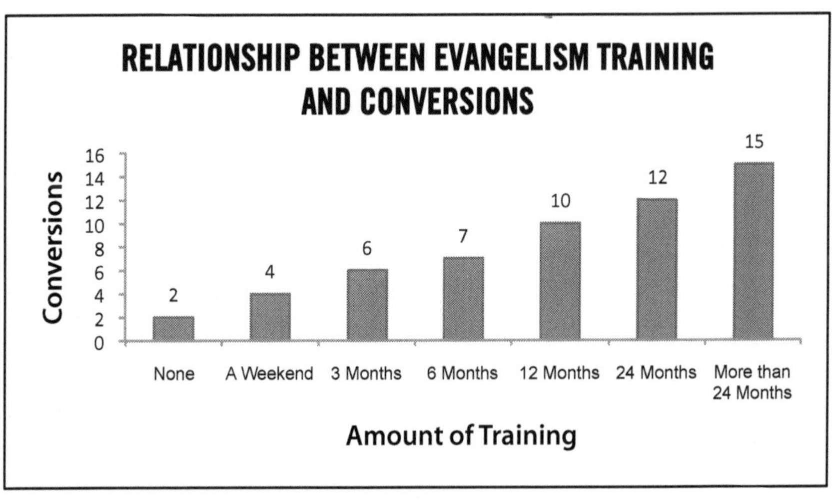

However, those were not the findings at all. The actual numbers are represented in the following chart.

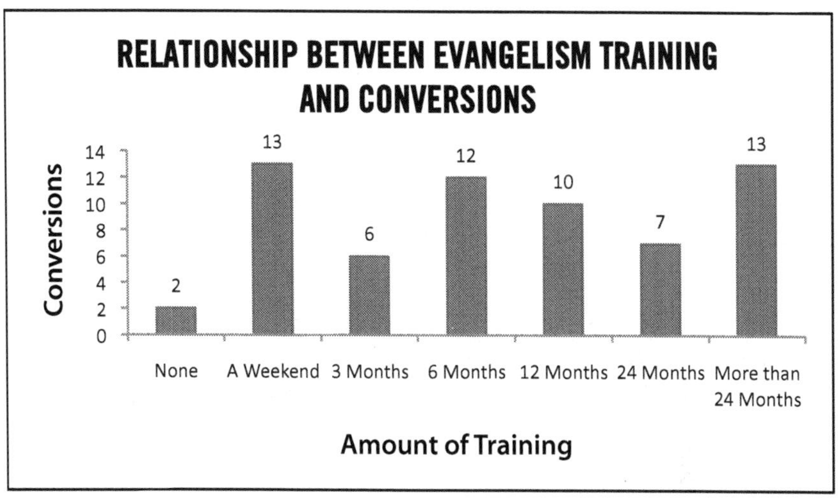

The data is a mess, isn't it? We can see that some evangelism training is better than none, but these results show no correlation between an increase in evangelism training and how many people that person will lead to Christ. A little surprising isn't it?

A related question brought even further insight. It examined not just how much training they had received, but whether they had been actively involved in an ongoing evangelism training program throughout the previous three years. We found that those who were involved led more than *twice* as many people to Christ as those who weren't.

Clearly, there is a relationship between involvement in an evangelism training program and how many people one leads to Christ. We have already seen that there is not a relationship between how *much* training one has received in evangelism and how many people one leads to Christ. So what's going on here? There must be something else that an evangelism training program provides besides knowledge and skills.

Survey participants were asked how many people they had shared the gospel with in the three preceding years. Those involved in an evangelism training program shared the gospel more than twice as often as those who were not involved in one. This would explain why people involved in evangelism training win twice as many people to Christ as those who aren't.

It's not that they know more. It's that they *share* more. Involvement in the program is providing them with things in addition to knowledge that help them share Christ on a more regular basis. Most of the programs I know of provide or require the following:

1. Vision casting from the program leaders
2. Example setting by the trainers
3. Prayer partners with a commitment to pray together weekly
4. Teamwork
5. Encouragement
6. Accountability
7. A specific time each week that is set aside for evangelism

These elements work together to spur the participants on "toward love and good deeds" (Hebrews 10:24), in this case, sharing the gospel. Think about this: How many of the things listed above can you receive from a sermon? Not many. What we really need is a team.

JOIN A TEAM

What do these findings say to us as disciple-makers? *Join a disciple-making team or an evangelism training program!* Winning someone to Christ is just the first step in the discipling process, but it is where laborers most often stumble when attempting to multiply their lives. Becoming part of a team that evangelizes together is the most important thing you can do if you want to multiply. Did you get that? It was a big one. Let me say it one more time. *Becoming part of a team that evangelizes together is the most important thing you can do if you want to multiply disciples, no matter where you are.*

As someone who believes in our utter dependence on God for fruit in evangelism, I would like to tell you that praying for the lost is the single most important thing you can do. Based on our research, however, that would not be accurate. Yes, praying for the lost is incredibly important, but remember, the disciples couldn't even watch and pray for one hour because their spirit was willing, but their flesh was weak. There is a greater likelihood that you will actually pray for the lost and act on those prayers if you are a part of a disciple-making team.

Just because Christians get together doesn't mean they will actually "spur each other on to love and good deeds" or function as a disciple-making team. Don't just join a small group. The church is full of inwardly focused small groups that do very little to help their members make disciples. Many list outreach as one of their purposes. Honestly though, I have never found a traditional church small group that kept outreach as a priority. The groups that do the best job of both helping their members grow and multiplying disciples are the groups that meet for the express purpose of being a disciple-making team. Their outward focus raises all the right issues and pushes all the right buttons for inward growth. This is one of those paradoxes of the kingdom. Groups focused on giving their lives away end up gaining life the most for themselves.[13]

NEVER QUIT

We all need to be a part of a disciple-making team, or at least an evangelism training program, that provides vision, a model, encouragement, coaching, teamwork, accountability, and prayer. One may graduate from a training program, but none of us ever graduate from needing a missional community that functions as a disciple-making team.

Years before I conducted this survey, I asked a few graduates of a well-known evangelism training program what they thought of the training. They answered with an enthusiastic "It's great!" Then, I asked them if they had consistently shared their faith after graduating from the program. The answer was the same with all of them: "Not really." This disturbed me, so I went to talk with one of the trainers of the program and asked him about this problem. He said, "Well, I think if they come back as trainers, they will gain more confidence and then they will share more consistently." Unfortunately, this was not correct. The determining factor seems to be whether or not someone is currently in a missional community that is spurring them on "toward love and good deeds." No wonder the next verse goes on to say we should "not give up meeting together as some are in the habit of doing" (NIV). This debunks the myth in disciple-making that Conviction (believing deeply that I should do something) + Competency (knowing how to do something) = Consistency. The old equation needs to be rewritten: Conviction + Competence + Community = Consistency.

If the closest thing you can find to a disciple-making team in your area is an evangelism training program, then join it and stay in it either as a trainee or trainer. Get it out of your head that you will ever graduate from it. You're not in it for the knowledge. You're in it for the teamwork, prayer, encouragement, structure, and accountability.

THE CHURCH AS A DISCIPLE-MAKING TEAM

Jesus did not build individual disciples. He didn't meet Peter before work at the Capernaum Starbucks for a one-on-one meeting and then meet John for a fish sandwich at the local seafood restaurant. Instead, he worked hard to build his followers into a disciple-making team. Jesus' goal was never to build individual disciples. He built a team and expected them to go build other disciple-making teams called churches.

Over the years, I have heard people say, "Jesus didn't command us to plant churches, he commanded us to make disciples. We should just make disciples and let him build his church like he said he would." On first hearing, that kind of sounds right, doesn't it? It gives that impression because it references two well-known statements of Jesus—"make disciples" and "I will build my church." The problem, though, is that it totally ignores the context of Jesus' ministry in which he made those statements. The ministry model Jesus lived out for his men involved forming a community of believers that functioned together as a disciple-making team. Modeling is one of the most powerful teaching tools available. Jesus perfectly modeled the kind of ministry he wanted his disciples to engage in when he left. We know that they caught what he was doing because after he left, they went and formed communities of disciple-makers wherever they went. Furthermore, the Holy Spirit inspired Paul to write his teammates specific instructions about the intentional forming of these communities (churches).[14]

After years of living and interacting with other cultures, I think that only an American could conceive of an individualistic, one-on-one approach to disciple-making. Most other cultures seem to know instinctively that we cannot and should not even try to multiply disciples alone. If we are going to multiply disciples, we must intentionally multiply disciple-making communities in which they can live and minister. Attempting to multiply individual disciples and not disciple-making teams will inevitably result in failure and frustration.

Sadly, few churches function as disciple-making teams, even though Jesus built the first New Testament church and gave the command to his followers to go "make disciples."[15] In your community, you may find churches that look like and function as a number of different things—social clubs, entertainment centers, lecture halls, or social service centers. Unfortunately, it is hard to find one functioning as a disciple-making movement. In many cities, if you want to be a part of a disciple-making team, you are going to have to join a para-church ministry. I praise God for para-church ministries, but I long for the day that it is easy to find a local church functioning as a disciple multiplying movement. Regretfully, this basic role of the church is neither understood nor expected today. We have lost a biblical idea of what it means to be a follower of Christ. Our definition nowadays of what it means to be a Christian has been reduced to avoiding stuff: don't get drunk, don't commit adultery, don't lie. Jesus didn't say, "Come, follow me and don't do stuff." No, he said, "Come, follow me and I will make you fishers of men" (Matthew 4:19). Following involves fishing. If you are not fishing, you are not following. Churches are supposed to help their members be successful at catching fish and helping those fish mature and multiply. This is clear in Scripture.

> And he gave the apostles, the prophets, the evangelists, the shepherds and teachers, *to equip the saints for the work of ministry,* for building up the body of Christ... (Ephesians 4:11-12)

Church leaders should equip the saints to do the work of ministry. We need a new measure of success for churches. The current one seems to be that a church is successful if it is increasing in numbers. There are many reasons a church could increase in numbers that may have nothing to do with its members doing ministry, multiplying themselves spiritually, or maturing in the faith. Good preaching and a talented band can attract people and make a church's attendance increase. New neighborhoods going in nearby or trouble at another church in the area can also make a church grow. Numerical growth from these sources can sometimes mask how unhealthy a church is and its failure to multiply mature disciples. Rather than asking the question "Are we growing?" we need to ask, "Are our members leading people to Christ?" and "Are they successfully helping new converts grow into mature believers?"

INCOMPLETE DEFINITIONS OF CHURCH

We need to redefine what it means to be a healthy church. I have heard campus ministries tell their graduating seniors that they need to join a good church wherever they end up. The definition given or implied of a good church usually includes:

- They preach the Bible.
- They are doctrinally sound.
- They have small groups.
- They believe in and support missions.

Not stated, but assumed in the definition are:

- They are financially sound.
- They are not undergoing a split or power struggle.

What's missing? We don't even notice. Are they making disciples? How could something as basic as this be missing from the list of characteristics of a healthy church? It's just not expected that one can find a church where the pastors and elders are actually engaged in multiplying disciples. Teaching small group Bible studies? Sure, but there is a world of difference between leading a Bible study and leading a team of people into whom you are pouring your life and with whom you are working to evangelize and multiply. Many pastors speak and teach about making disciples. I wonder what would happen though if one Sunday morning they stopped their sermon and asked the men they were discipling to come up and join them on stage. Would anyone come up? Would they have stories to tell of how their pastor didn't just teach them a Bible study, but actually did life and ministry together with them?

HOW DID WE GET HERE?

How did we get to the point that we don't even expect our church leaders to be models of multiplication like Paul and Timothy? "And the things you have heard me say in the presence of many witnesses entrust to reliable men who will also be qualified to teach others" (2 Timothy 2:2, NIV). How did we lose the idea that the church should function as a disciple-making movement that helps its members bear fruit in evangelism and discipleship? (See Ephesians 4:11-12.) Why would we leave this off from our list of characteristics of a healthy church? I have an idea. When I was a college student, I would work construction for my brother during the term breaks. As the "college boy" on the construction site, I was often given the grunt work. I remember one day it started to rain. A foreman took me into a shack and handed me a stake used to hold the foundation's form. He pointed to a pile of scrap wood and told me to cut it into stakes like the one he handed me. It was the standard I was to use to make other stakes. Since this job was better than being out in the rain and digging footers, I happily put on my headphones, jammed out to some music, and began turning scrap wood into useful stakes. There was only one problem. After a while it became clear that something had gone wrong. The stake he handed me as a model was two feet long. After using it to measure where to cut the next stake, I threw it down and used the new stake to measure the next piece of wood. Using this method, I was actually losing about a quarter of an inch each time. After a while, the stakes I was cutting were pretty short. Each stake only fell a little short of its predecessor. The lessening of the standard happened so incrementally that it was virtually unnoticeable unless you went back to the original model and compared. In the same way, our churches don't look unhealthy when we compare them to other churches around us or to our immediate predecessors. But when we compare them to the church Jesus planted and the churches in the book of Acts, we have to use hermeneutical gymnastics and creative missiology to explain why our churches don't resemble those and yet are still considered "healthy."

THE CORE MESSAGE

I want to share with you an email I sent to a friend that I believe summarizes the core message I hope will stick with you:

> I believe that *the single greatest determining factor* as to whether people multiply themselves is *not* the level of their maturity, the amount of training they have received, the receptivity of the lost in their context

or how long they have been discipled. But it is whether or not they are *immersed in a disciple-making team.*

Wherever you find people multiplying themselves, you will find that they are a part of a ministry that provides them with certain things like:

- Top leaders who both cast the vision of multiplying *and* model it
- Ongoing coaching or mentoring
- Macro (large) ministry events that are designed to help the disciple-maker's micro ministry
- A ministry culture that expects, prays for, and works together to multiply

If multiplication is taking place, you will find these elements. You will find them in church planting movements, wildly growing cell churches, multiplying campus ministries, and disciple-making churches. Jesus did not just help his disciples grow in maturity and learn ministry skills. Often, that is what we think is involved in disciple-making. Therefore we think we can do it one-on-one over coffee. What we miss is the fact that *Jesus built a disciple-making community*. A relatively immature Christ-follower who is a part of a disciple-making team has a far better chance of multiplying disciples than a mature believer who is separated from a team. Jesus never intended for any of his disciples to try to make disciples solo. Come be a part of the team!

If these elements are so essential for multiplication, it is crucial that we understand how to identify, engage in, and cultivate each one of them. Since our future impact depends on them, we will unpack each one in the next chapter.

CHAPTER 5

ESSENTIAL ELEMENTS

Rachel just graduated from college. She took a job in her state's capital city. She knew she needed to find a good church, but she wasn't really sure how she should pick a new fellowship. Beyond sound doctrine, what should she look for? What type of church would help her succeed at multiplying disciples?

Ryan and Emily started a small group for newlyweds three years ago with the vision that it would grow and multiply. After two and a half years of Bible study and fellowship with other couples, they realized no one in their group had led a single person to Christ. They ended the group and are now wondering what they should do differently if they start a new one. There are lots of things they could do, but what are the essentials that will create a context in which their members will flourish in personal ministry?

Cory just graduated from seminary. The church where he has been serving as youth director just offered him the senior pastor job starting in two months when the current pastor retires. In seminary, Cory studied factors that make churches grow in size. He is aware attendance growth can be a result of a number of different influences—being located in a growing suburb, transfer growth because another church is having problems, cool music, good preaching, etc. But Cory is wrestling with a significant question. What is needed to help individual believers succeed at multiplying their lives? He doesn't just want to grow his church's attendance. His dream is to build and unleash an army of equipped laborers into the world to expand the kingdom of God to every nation, tribe, and tongue. But what does he need to do to see his church transformed into a laborer-producing movement? What type of environment does he need to create?

Botanists tell us that all ninety or so naturally-occurring elements may be found in normal plant tissue. How many of these are actually essential for healthy plant growth and reproduction? Only sixteen! In our disciple-making research, we wrestled with this issue of essentiality. One can find a huge variety of ministry practices in churches, ministries, and small groups. Which of these practices are absolutely essential for spiritual growth and reproduction? We wanted to know what Rachel should look for in a church, what essential elements Ryan and Emily should build into their small group, and how Cory could transform his church into a laborer-producing movement. What is truly essential?

NON-ESSENTIAL ELEMENTS

One of the best ways to find the essential is to remove the non-essential. We found the following things were not important in determining the effectiveness of one's disciple-making:

- Where you live
- The number of lost people with whom you work closely on a daily basis
- The age or size of your church
- Attending a church that holds seeker style worship service[16] (Seeker services may draw crowds and help people come to Christ, but they don't help the individual believer in the pew increase effectiveness in multiplying themself spiritually.)
- Your age (You can't be too young or too old!)
- How many children you have (Even people with a bunch of kids can multiply disciples!)

Additionally, Joel Comiskey's definitive work on understanding group growth finds that you don't have to be an extrovert or have the gift of evangelism to multiply your cell group.[17] What encouragement to those of us who are introverts or who don't have the gift of evangelism! Now that we have looked at a few things you don't need, let's look at some you do.

THE ESSENTIALS

Whether you are trying to lead your small group into becoming a disciple-making team or attempting to lead a bunch of teams as a movement, understanding the context you need to create is crucial. The presence of these elements will increase the effectiveness of those you lead.

1. THE LEADER CHAMPIONS THE VISION OF SPIRITUAL MULTIPLICATION CONSTANTLY.

The top leader of any organization defines why it exists. There is little chance that any church or small group will develop a disciple-making culture if spiritual multiplication is not central in the vision of the leader and frequently on his lips. In fact, 51 percent of the disciple-makers who scored as effective in our study reported that their leader championed the vision on a *weekly* basis. Only 3 percent of effective disciple-makers said that their leader never championed the vision.

Casting vision is a process, not an event. With the world, the flesh, and satanic forces ever eager to cloud our vision, we need to hear it again and again. Consider Jesus casting perspective with Peter. In Matthew, Jesus approached Peter and challenged him to something bigger than his next meal: "Follow me, and I will make you fishers of men" (Matthew 4:19). Jesus then modeled for Peter a life of fishing for men and women, not just from his own nation, but from other nations, too.

Peter witnessed Jesus talking with Romans (Matthew 8:5-13) and Samaritans (John 4:1-42), not just Jews. After three years of hearing and watching the vision lived out before him, Peter should have understood that the goal was to make disciples *of all nations*, right? Just in case three years of watching Jesus live the vision was not enough, Christ cast the vision again after his resurrection in John 20:21, "As the Father has sent me, even so I am sending you." It wasn't until after Jesus left, though, that the fog rolled in on Peter. He quickly went back to fishing for fish and not men (John 21:1-3). Thankfully, Jesus patiently recast the vision for Peter, telling him to "feed my sheep" (John 21:17).

Now Peter was back on track. Jesus could quit sharing the vision, right? Apparently the master disciple-maker didn't think so. He presented the mission again in his final words, making it clear that Peter and the other disciples were to make disciples of *all nations* (Matthew 28:18-20). And again, in case they still didn't get it, Jesus told them their ministry should extend to people beyond Judea, into Samaria and to the "end of the earth" (Acts 1:8). Peter still didn't get it. In Acts 10, the Lord had to put Peter in a trance, show him a shocking dream, and send men to go lead him into cross-cultural ministry.

If Peter, who was discipled directly by Jesus, needed to hear the vision that frequently, then so do we. We need to get ourselves into communities where we will hear our mission talked about again and again and again. Leaders, when you are sick of hearing yourself cast the vision, do it again, work it into another sermon, or joyfully declare it as the focus of your church or group when you make announcements.

Our goal is not merely to instill purpose in individual disciples. A dream that endures and grows is one shared in community. Notice the "thems" in the following verses.

> And he said to *them*, "Follow me, and I will make you fishers of men." (Matthew 4:19)

> And Jesus came and said to *them*, "All authority in heaven and on earth has been given to me. Go therefore and make disciples of all nations…" (Matthew 28:18-19)

> He said to *them*… "But you will receive power when the Holy Spirit has come upon you, and you will be my witnesses in Jerusalem and in all Judea and Samaria, and to the end of the earth." (Acts 1:7-8)

We need to help our community come to share a common purpose and passion. Though we might cast the vision frequently, we will never be able to cast it frequently enough. We need to develop a community that consistently "spurs one another on toward love and good deeds" (Hebrews 10:24 NIV). People need encouragement to walk with the Lord and live out their purpose on a *daily* basis (Hebrews 3:13). Only a *community* of believers can provide that kind of frequency. But how do communities that dream big get started? Their leaders prime the pump and never quit dripping the vision.

2. THE LEADER MODELS THE VISION OF SPIRITUAL MULTIPLICATION.

Our survey asked people if their leaders modeled spiritual multiplication. Many people answered "Don't Know" on this question, which was essentially saying, "Maybe my leader did, but I didn't see it." Eighty-three percent of these people were non-effective. In contrast, 84 percent of effective disciple-makers said yes, they did see their leaders model spiritual multiplication. This sent off our software's alarm bells, indicating we had found something significant. Apparently it is pretty hard to live out a challenging vision when you don't see your leaders doing it!

This research finding was no surprise. Paul stressed this very point to his young protégé, Titus, when he exhorted him to "show yourself in all respects to be a model of good works..." (Titus 2:7). It is hard to imagine a situation where believers are actively multiplying themselves spiritually though their pastor or small group leader is not. Ministry leaders must both speak the vision *and* live it out in front of their people. When people hear you talk, they listen. When people see you do, they do. Maybe we should call this "The monkey see, monkey do principle"! Why should we expect people to do what we're not doing?

The research is clear: leaders who model the vision for their people help them increase their effectiveness. By itself, this is a significant finding. But coupled together with the relationship we saw between effectiveness and vision casting by the leader, we have an unmistakable message that leaders must lead the charge in disciple-making, both in word and deed. (See note to pastors in Appendix 1.)

Leaders, do you have a few key people into whom you are actively pouring your life? Are they close enough to you to see how you live and minister? Do they see you sharing your faith on a regular basis? We should never expect the people we lead to multiply if they don't see us modeling personal ministry.

3. THE CHURCH OR MINISTRY FREQUENTLY OFFERS MINISTRY TRAINING GEARED TOWARD HELPING MEMBERS MULTIPLY.

Effective disciple-makers are involved with churches or small groups that offer regular training that is aimed at equipping them to do the work of the ministry. You can tell a lot about a church or ministry by the training they do or don't offer. You see, there are two very different paradigms under which churches and ministries operate. One paradigm says, "We'll do the spiritual ministry, and you help us by bringing people, working the nursery, parking cars, and praying for us." The other paradigm comes straight from Ephesians 4:11-12 and says, "We exist to help you successfully multiply yourself." And I find these two very different approaches to ministry not just in churches but in campus ministries as well. I visited a college campus recently and spent time learning about six of the different ministries on campus. In interviewing their students and staff, one of the things I was looking for was which ministry philosophy they had adopted. Sadly, it seems that only one of the six ministries was operating under the equipping paradigm.

Wherever you find disciples exponentially multiplying, you will find an emphasis on training. This is true in church planting movements. David Garrison, in his book *Church Planting Movements*, reports on wildly multiplying networks of churches around the world. Here are a few examples of the multiplication that is taking place.

> SOUTHEAST ASIA
>
> When a strategy coordinator began his assignment in 1993, there were only three churches and eighty-five believers among a population of more than 7 million lost souls. Four years later, there were more than 550 churches and nearly 55,000 believers.
>
> NORTH AFRICA
>
> In his weekly Friday sermon, an Arab Muslim cleric complained that more than 10,000 Muslims living in the surrounding mountains had apostatized from Islam and become Christians.
>
> CITY IN CHINA
>
> Over a four-year period (1993-1997), more than 20,000 people came to faith in Christ, resulting in more than 500 new churches.
>
> LATIN AMERICA
>
> Two Baptist unions overcame significant government persecution to grow from 235 churches in 1990 to more than 3,200 in 1998.
>
> CENTRAL ASIA
>
> A strategy coordinator reports, "Around the end of 1996, we called around to the various churches in the area and got their count on how many had come to faith in that one year. When they were all added up,

> it came to 15,000 in one year. The previous year we estimated only 200 believers altogether."
>
> WESTERN EUROPE
>
> A missionary in Europe reports, "Last year (1998), my wife and I started 15 new church cell groups. As we left for a six-month stateside assignment last July, we wondered what we'd find when we returned. It's wild! We can verify at least 30 churches now, but I believe that it could be two or even three times that many."
>
> ETHIOPIA
>
> A missionary strategist commented, "It took us 30 years to plant four churches in this country. We've started 65 cell churches in the last nine months."[18]

One of the common elements that Garrison reports finding in these movements is on-the-job training. And the way ministry training is presented in these contexts is not just "Let us train you how to minister," but rather the more multiplication-minded approach of "Let us train you how to *train others*."

When looking for a church that offers training, please realize that not everything called "training" actually is. I recently saw an announcement in a church bulletin offering a "training" session for new small group leaders. It was really just lecture-style teaching in a classroom. Is that the kind of thing I am encouraging you to look for when selecting a church? It might look like it on the surface, but a little deeper digging reveals a few things about this church that tells me they are falling short of operating as a disciple-making movement.

- While their pastor talks about making disciples and leads a couple of Bible studies for men, he is not personally pouring his life into a few and doing practical ministry together with them. He is modeling being a teacher, but not an evangelist/discipler/trainer /coach.
- The purpose of small groups at this church is for Bible study and fellowship, not multiplication. What they don't understand is that people grow the most when they are on mission together. Groups focused on multiplication, not on personal growth, see their members

grow and mature at a quicker rate. Missional teams study the Bible, fellowship, and pray, too. But the focus on mission instead of just team members' growth provides a healthy motivation and balance in their growth and community.

- It is great that they are offering this class for someone who is interested in leading a small group, but unfortunately there is no *ongoing* training for their leaders. Our research shows that receiving ministry training on a *weekly* basis is what most increases effectiveness in disciple-making. We found that 48.5 percent of highly effective disciple-makers were involved with churches or ministries that offered weekly ministry training. This was true of only 29.8 percent of non-effective disciple-makers.
- The chief way someone is trained to lead in this church is through a class. But in multiplying ministries that successfully train people to reproduce, the focus is on apprenticeship to existing leaders, not classes.
- They have no coaching system for their leaders.

I hope you are catching some of the important differences between churches and ministries that function as disciple-making movements and those that don't. Your future impact depends on it!

4. MEMBERS OF THE CHURCH OR SMALL GROUP ENGAGE IN GIVING AND RECEIVING REGULAR COACHING.

Training involves showing a person or group how to do something. Coaching usually follows training and involves the coach giving feedback and ideas for improvement while the game or work is in progress. Jesus coached his disciples in their ministry successes and failures. For example, during his debriefing with the seventy-two (Luke 10:17) after they returned from their short-term mission trip, he helped them interpret their success. He gave a better cause for rejoicing than demons submitting to them, namely that their names were written in the Lamb's book of life. When the disciples failed in attempting to heal a paralytic (Matthew 17:14-21), Jesus was there to help them interpret the cause of their failure (lack of faith) and coach them on what success in the future would take (prayer and fasting). Paul wrote to Timothy and Titus as a part of his coaching them in their ministry assignments. It should be no surprise that we found that highly effective disciple-makers received ministry coaching.

Survey participants were questioned regarding how frequently they had received coaching during the three-year period our study investigated. Nearly three quarters (74.9 percent) of those who had not received any coaching were found to be non-effective. That percentage dropped to 26.1 percent for those who had received coaching every other month. Receiving coaching is clearly beneficial for those who wish to multiply their lives. We can all benefit from the wisdom, encouragement, and accountability of an experienced mentor.

When looking for a church to join, it is important to ask whether they have a coaching system in place for those who want to multiply their lives. In my experience, most of the churches that have well defined coaching structures are built on a cell model. Though these churches vary some in the exact implementation of their coaching structure, basically they are set up so that everyone gets the feedback and advice they need to succeed. For example, I ate breakfast a few years ago with a senior pastor and the twelve men that he coached. During the meeting, each man reported on how the men they were leading were doing, and the senior pastor gave advice when needed. These men would in turn meet with their men and coach them, and so on down the multiplication chain. When coaching is taken seriously and done consistently, everyone benefits, multiplication occurs, and the church grows. Many cell churches with well-developed coaching strategies have grown into hundreds of thousands of members, and the growth has come from equipping their members to do the work of the ministry, not from having the slickest preacher or best music.

I realize that when I speak of looking for a church or ministry that has a well-developed coaching system, some readers, especially younger ones, may react negatively because a group that has carefully organized systems doesn't sound very "organic."[19] It may sound kind of mechanical and unnatural, maybe more like a business than a family. And that's not good, right? I'm with you. I want my church to look, feel, and function like a family and not a business. Unfortunately, many churches are more like corporations, and they turn me off, too. The truth, though, is that organisms in nature grow and flourish when they have healthy systems at work behind the scenes. Think for a minute about how our bodies need systems. We need our skeletal system, digestive system, nervous system, endocrine system, immune system, circulatory system, etc. Healthy families, at least the ones I've seen, have structure, systems, and coaching, and the kids in them flourish. If you find a group that just wants to be "organic" and unstructured, I wouldn't recommend joining it. It will probably not be healthy for long.

We need our systems to work well if we are going to grow and multiply. If a church or ministry talks multiplication but doesn't organize itself with that end in mind (doesn't develop a strong coaching system), talk and dreams are probably as far as that group will ever get. I am aware of many churches that desire to see their members make disciples and multiply. In some of these churches, you will even find pockets of reproduction. But to see effective disciple-making throughout a whole church requires a well-developed system of coaching. Dave and Jon Ferguson, who lead a movement of multiplying disciples and churches, put it this way: "Developing coaches (leaders of leaders) may be the single most overlooked yet vital task in spreading a missional movement."[20] I want you to immerse yourself in a *culture of multiplication*, and you won't find those where a deep commitment to coaching doesn't exist.

5. THE CHURCH'S OR MINISTRY'S SMALL GROUPS FUNCTION AS DISCIPLE-MAKING TEAMS.

Highly effective disciple-makers average twice as much time discussing evangelism, praying for the lost, and actually doing evangelism together with others in their small group as non-effective disciple-makers. Effective disciple-makers fall somewhere between the two. The relationship here is clear: increased time doing evangelistic activities together as a team increases effectiveness.

Most groups that function well as a disciple-making team define multiplication as their reason for existence. What we call a group is important because its name implies its reason for existence. Bible studies, fellowships, and prayer groups don't usually multiply. "Cells" multiply. "Evangelism Teams" multiply. "Disciple-Making Teams" multiply. Many churches start small groups for the purpose of assimilation and care. The best groups I have ever seen at assimilation and care, though, are those that form for the purpose of equipping and mobilizing their members. The church is supposed to build laborers, not hospitals. It is true that armies build hospitals and care for their people, but that's not the principle around which they organize. What should you do to apply this information? Join or start a movement that organizes its people into disciple-making teams that average twenty-five to thirty minutes each week doing each of the following activities:

- Discussing evangelism
- Praying for the lost
- Doing something evangelistic

Michael Stewart, Pastor of Missional Community at The Austin Stone Community Church, conveys the importance of pursuing mission within the context of community: "This wonderful, beautiful community we find in Acts 2 was a direct result of pursuing Jesus and his mission. At Austin Stone, we have realized that when you aim for Acts 2 community, you will get neither community nor mission. But if you aim to pursue Jesus and his mission, you'll get both mission and community."[21] Small group leader, are you leading a study or a disciple-making team?

6. THE CHURCH OR MINISTRY REGULARLY OFFERS EVANGELISTIC EVENTS.

Offering regular evangelistic events is important to supplement individual evangelistic efforts. While holding frequent evangelistic meetings doesn't mean that a church or ministry functions as a disciple-making movement, it seems that doing so can be an important component of a movement. Though these meetings can be helpful, caution must be used. Many times an emphasis on church-wide evangelistic events detracts from helping members be successful in their individual multiplication ministries.

It would be helpful to make two distinctions here in the way I have seen disciple-making ministries and non-disciple-making ministries view evangelistic meetings.

- Non-disciple-making ministries tend to do evangelism in large-group settings. Disciple-making ministries focus on equipping their members to do evangelism in smaller settings, like one-on-one discussions, small group Bible studies or cells.

- Disciple-making ministries might hold large group evangelistic events, but the decision to do so is driven out of asking the question, "How can we help our people be successful in their personal multiplication ministries?" Strategically timed and planned large outreach events can be very helpful to those who are actively working to multiply. In the disciple-making mindset, programming must always serve the needs of the individuals doing multiplication ministry and not the other way around.

7. THOSE SEEKING TO MULTIPLY ARE CHARACTERIZED BY ABUNDANT PRAYER.

There is a clear relationship between prayer for the lost and disciple-making effectiveness. Some of the most vibrant and effective multiplication-based churches I have ever visited are in South Korea. I have been in their *daily* 5:00 a.m. prayer meetings. They also hold *all night* prayer meetings and go on retreats to fast and pray for the lost for days, even weeks, at a time. Seem impossible?

When David Garrison studied fast growing church planting movements, which grow by training laypeople to multiply, he found that abundant prayer was not just a common element, it was *universal* in every movement.[22] I was visiting recently with a missionary trainer who spoke of the prayer habits he had witnessed in several church planting movements. He said, "These guys are spending crazy amounts of time in prayer *every day*." I don't know about you, but where I live, the idea of getting together with others every day and praying really would be considered a crazy idea. Who has time for that? Certainly that is going overboard and is not something God desires of us, right? Wrong. In the book of Acts we read:

> And they devoted themselves to the apostles' teaching and the fellowship, to the breaking of bread and the prayers. And awe came upon every soul, and many wonders and signs were being done through the apostles. And all who believed were together and had all things in common... And the Lord added to their number day by day those who were being saved. (Acts 2:42 – 47)

When it comes to prayer effectiveness, we reap in accordance with what we sow. If we want to reap daily, we need to sow daily. Maybe people back then lived differently, with simpler lifestyles and more time for prayer, right? Wrong again. Most spent their days working for their next meal. We spend hours each day watching television, surfing the internet, playing sports, managing money, and other stuff. I don't think they had more time each day than we do. The Koreans who get up and pray every day don't have more time to pray than we do either. So what's the difference? Could it be we just don't *want* to pray? Ouch! If I'm honest, it's often true for me. Why? When prayer becomes just what we have to do to get stuff, it becomes a chore. It gets put onto our "to do" list or our set of goals, along with other things like "Lose 10 pounds." Most of us don't enjoy working down a "to do" list.

Something you will notice if you have the privilege of getting immersed in a multiplication culture where prayer is abundant and natural is that a passion for Jesus and his kingdom is what leads people to their knees. They view prayer as fellowship with the Father and not as a "to do" item or a goal or a chore. Want to multiply your life? Look for people who are passionate about God and love to fellowship with him in prayer. Begin to intentionally hang out with them. You'll soon find yourself praying a lot more and enjoying it!

We must remember, though, prayer alone is not enough to help people be effective disciple-makers. Prayer must be accompanied by other activities which are found in Scripture. We must get the essential elements working together simultaneously.

OTHER HELPFUL FACTORS

There are a couple of other elements that may not be absolutely essential but are very beneficial. You will find them in Scripture and in most disciple-making movements.

1. RETREATS

Jesus frequently took his disciples away for focused times of interaction, teaching, prayer, and rest. Almost every fruitful disciple-making ministry I have seen makes effective use of strategically timed ministry retreats. Sometimes these are designed to be evangelistic in nature. Other times they are aimed at helping new disciples deal with junk in their past and find freedom in Christ or to cast the vision of disciple-making. At times, they are large events utilizing conference centers, and other times they are small, lakeside cabin experiences. I personally have seen spiritual growth and relationship deepening, that otherwise would have taken months, happen in a weekend at a mountain cabin getaway. Rich times together in the Word and prayer take place in a way that seems to rarely happen in the flow of daily life. Why not plan a retreat for your small group in the next month or two?

2. INSPIRING LARGE GROUP EVENTS

When I was a rookie campus minister, I inherited a disciple-making ministry from a very gifted predecessor named Mike. The Lord blessed Mike and his female staff partner's ministry on this very small college campus. They held weekly large group ministry events that were aimed at evangelizing the lost, casting ministry vision, and generally challenging new disciples to walk with God. These meetings drew upwards of 200 students. The ministry happening on a personal level was equally impressive. The staff members discipled key men and women, usually seniors. These key men and women discipled juniors, who in turn discipled sophomores. And some of the sophomores discipled freshmen. Mike and his partner also held biweekly leaders' meetings for training and coaching the leaders in the movement.

After a semester of following Mike's ministry pattern, I decided that I would tweak the approach to take the movement to the next level. I reasoned, "If we can make our disciple-makers more effective, our ministry will grow both in depth and breadth." My idea of how to do this was to increase the frequency of our leadership training. Because I was concerned about adding a weekly leaders' meeting to their already full schedules, I decided I would just turn our current new disciples meeting into a leadership training time. I taught on topics like "How to select disciples" and "How to build convictions in your disciples." It wasn't long before our attendance numbers began to plummet. My initial response was, "That's okay. If we make our disciple-makers more successful, we will be better off in the long run." Soon after, though, I realized that I had underestimated the value of our large group events to the disciple-making process. Those large group events that cast the vision and challenged disciples to walk with God were actually a way that we partnered with our leaders and helped reinforce what they were doing on the micro level with the people they discipled.

Jesus had a relational ministry with twelve, but this did not cause him to ignore the masses. He continued to evangelize them and cast the vision of the kingdom to them.[23] There are contexts in the world today where large meetings are impossible. However, I believe that the same benefits can be achieved if two or more cells or house churches come together. We should not underestimate the importance of the vision building, momentum, and unity that this creates. How about getting your group together with other disciple-making teams sometime soon to cast vision and challenge your members?

Just to be clear, I am only advocating large group events that are specifically planned with the purpose of partnering with disciple-makers and helping them be successful in their relational ministries. Many large group events are simply planned as an end in themselves. There are tons of churches and ministries that just love to do big events. These frequently are very impressive, draw big crowds, and at the end of the day do very little to help advance the multiplication of disciples. In fact, in many cases they require so much preparation time that they use up all of the time and energy resources of potential disciple-makers, hurting their personal efforts to multiply. Successful multiplication movements work to protect the time of their disciple-makers and make sure that macro events serve micro ministries.

In the next chapters, we will shift our focus away from characteristics of the ministries that highly effective disciple-makers live in and look at the personal behaviors and approaches to ministry of people who multiply. Before you move on, though, take a minute to look over the following table. Could it be a tool to evaluate churches you are considering joining? Might pastors like Cory use it to help them plan and evaluate their ministries? Small group leaders, could this be a guide for your ministry? Don't let it intimidate you. Remember, you should engage in ministry together with others as a team. Your teammates can help where you are weak, and it is in your weakness that God displays his strength!

ELEMENT	WEAK	AVERAGE	STRONG
Vision Casting			
Modeling			
Ministry Training			
Coaching			
Small Groups are Teams			
Evangelistic Events			
Abundant Prayer			
Retreats			
Inspiring Events			

Part 3

Effective Disciple-Making Practices

James and Carl attended the same church for five years. They are fortunate men. Their church was made up of many disciple-making teams functioning together as a movement. The culture of their church truly supported the personal ministry efforts of their members. James and many others in the church saw their ministries explode in just a few years. Carl, on the other hand, saw little fruit for all his efforts. He had the same advantages of being immersed in a disciple-making movement as James. So what was the difference? Our research found that highly effective disciple-makers not only immerse themselves in helpful contexts, they also engage in certain ministry practices that set them apart. It was the combination of helpful environments *and* these practices that enabled them to see extraordinary results. The following chapters will examine these biblical behaviors.

THE MULTIPLICATION CYCLE

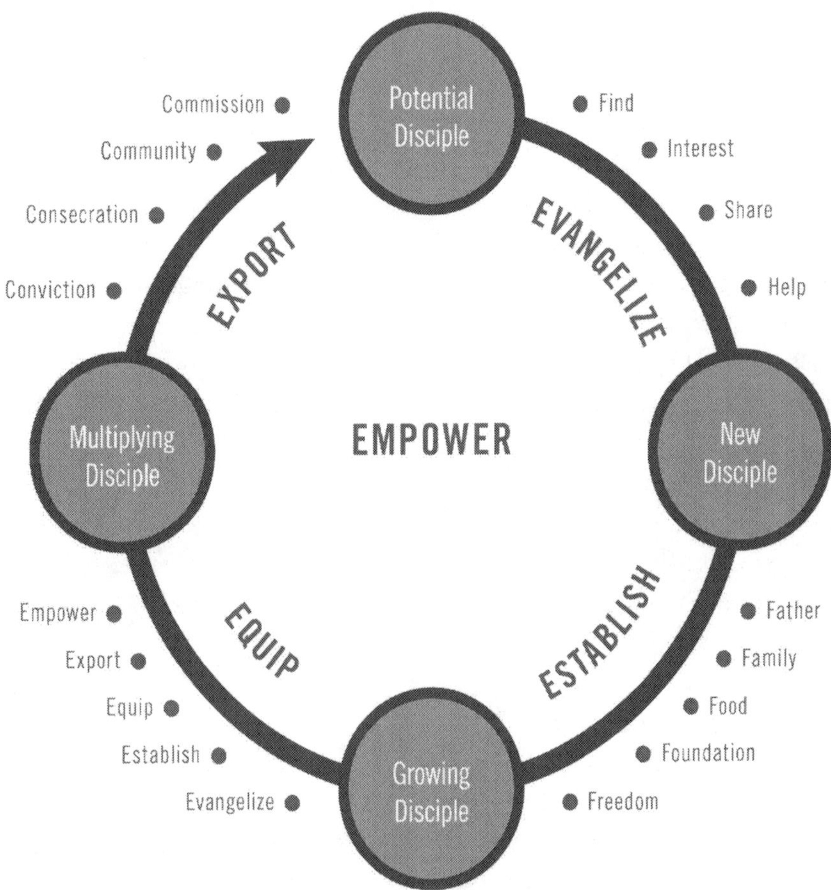

Many churches and ministries have found it helpful to create grids that outline the disciple-making cycle. The diagram above is one I created to capture much of the process. It can be a useful tool for you in teaching and evaluating your disciple-making practices.

CHAPTER 6

GONE FISHING

[EVANGELIZING]

One hot and humid Bangkok evening in the summer of 1987, my new Thai friend named Nok invited me to go fishing with him. My first reaction was, "Are you kidding me? We are in the middle of a concrete jungle; where are we going to go fishing around here?" I was used to fishing in Florida bays and Alabama farm ponds. I couldn't imagine where we would fish in that metropolis of millions. Much to my surprise, later that evening I had my hook in the water. We had not left the city. Sprinkled throughout Bangkok are stocked fishing ponds. These ponds are surrounded by crudely made pavilions with palm branch roofs. Inside the pavilion you find a table for your gear and maybe for eating and drinking if you should decide to order something. A loud clap of the hands will bring a young boy on a bicycle to take your order. Several chairs for you and your friends round out the pavilion furnishings. In America, fishing is a quiet and solitary sport, but in Thailand, it has been turned into a social event!

If you actually catch something, you have two options: take the fish to the kitchen and have them cook it for you, or sell it back to the pond owners. The Thai fishing experience definitely was not what I was used to. It wasn't just the surroundings that were different. It seemed like everything about fishing in Thailand was different from fishing in Alabama. The fish were not three-pound bass; they were forty pound monsters. When you caught one, it would often take twenty minutes or longer to reel it in. The hooks didn't have an eye to put your line through, so I had to learn a new way of tying a hook. The bait we used wasn't worms or crickets or shrimp. Instead we used sticky rice.

When Thais eat sticky rice, they pick up some with their hands, squeeze it together into a ball, and then dip it into sauce. But using it for bait is a two step process. First, you make a small, firm ball about the size of a rubber bouncy ball, and you put your hook into it. Then you pack more sticky rice, a bit more loosely, around that ball. The result is an end product about the size of a baseball. This outer layer is meant to come off easily and attract the interest of the fish. Hopefully, trying a bit of it will convince the fish to bite down harder on the firm ball inside and run with it. Once you have the interest-creating outer layer packed on just right, you are ready to sling that honker out as far as you can.

The next step is to loosen the drag on your reel, lay your pole down carefully, or jam the handle into a crack in the dock and sit back and wait for a fish to pick it up and run with it. It really is quite exciting to have your conversation with your friend interrupted by the *Vvvvvvvvvvuuu* sound your reel makes when the fish starts to run with your bait. When you hear that sound and grab your pole, don't try to set the hook too quickly. If you do, you will lose the fish.

This whole experience made me feel like a ten-year-old on his first fishing trip all over again. The big difference between when my dad took me fishing in a stocked pond in North Carolina and fishing in Bangkok was that the fish in North Carolina were so hungry to eat that they almost jumped out of the water to bite my hook. The ones in Bangkok seemed really disinterested and hard to attract.

Three years later, I found myself back in Thailand, but this time fishing for men. Again, I was confronted by all the differences between Thailand and home. I was left feeling like I was fishing (for men) for the very first time. Over the next several years, my fishing buddies (my fellow missionary teammates) from America and I would have to learn some new ways of fishing. Some of you are preparing to graduate from college and enter the real world. You may have had some success fishing for men on campus, but will you continue to have success when you change ponds? Others of you are out in the real world and are discouraged because you have landed so few in the boat or maybe can't even get a bite. I have great news for you. It *is* possible to lead men and women to Christ in the real world. Many have proven it. Every day, all over the world, people are leading their family members, neighbors, coworkers, and even strangers to Christ. No doubt, some places are easier than others. In North Carolina, at the stocked pond, just about anybody with a pole could catch a fish. In Bangkok, however, you have to apply all the principles of good fishing if you are going to catch anything. I want to share some biblical principles of fishing with you that are trans-cultural and will work no matter what your context. You will have to figure out the specific applications for your particular situation, but I am confident the Holy Spirit will help you do so.

OVERLOOKED BIBLICAL PRINCIPLES OF EVANGELISM

Thailand is a great place to learn what doesn't work in evangelism. Protestant mission work has been going on there for more than 180 years, and still only one half of one percent of the population follow Christ. Young missionaries often discover that what works at home doesn't work in Thailand. They find out that what they thought were universal principles were actually cultural applications. In the case of our team, what we discovered was not that the tools in our bag didn't work, but that we needed tools we didn't even know existed. Failures in evangelism led us into Bible study and discussion about what we could possibly be missing. This journey led us to discover some very simple principles that we hadn't seen before or just didn't realize were important because it was easier to catch fish in our home pond. Now that I have lived back in the States for a number of years, I have seen that these principles definitely work here, too, and they have made me much more effective. They have also taken a lot of the stress and fear out of evangelism for me, and I believe they will for you too.

I have taught a course on disciple-making a number of times at a local seminary. When I get to the section on evangelism, I tell my students, "Welcome to the logjam in the multiplication cycle." I am convinced that most would be able to help people learn to walk with the Lord and multiply their lives if they could just lead people to Christ on a regular basis. If you don't, the whole multiplication process comes to a screeching halt. Before reading further, would you stop to pray and ask the Holy Spirit to reveal to you something that you may have overlooked, maybe something that I don't even mention, in your evangelism efforts?

OUR JOURNEY

When our long-term team first started to evangelize in Thailand, I instructed them not to waste a lot of time with people who were not interested in the gospel. There were so many millions of Thai people to be reached. How could we justify spending time with those who weren't even interested? As we studied language that first year, we would have occasions to share our faith. At first it had to be in English since all we could say in Thai was that we liked bananas or that it was hot. As we shared with people in English, it never seemed like we found much interest in the gospel. We desperately worked and struggled to learn Thai. We longed to be able to share the gospel with them in their heart language. Certainly we would see a better response when we could share in Thai.

When I neared the end of my formal language study, I took a couple of classes on biblical and spiritual vocabulary. Riding home one afternoon from language school in a taxi, I had an hour to share the gospel with the driver. I spoke passionately and prayerfully using all of my newly learned vocabulary. When I reached the end, I remember thinking, "That was the best job I've done at sharing the gospel since I moved here over a year ago. Certainly it will make an impact on this guy." His response was, "*Gall dee. Tuk sasanaa sawn hi khon ben khon dee.*" Which translates to, "That's good. Every religion teaches people to be good." Or maybe I should say that it translates to, "What you just said made absolutely no impact on me." I remember at that minute thinking, "Water off a duck's back! How could my best ever gospel presentation roll off of him like water off a duck's back?" You may be thinking now, sounds like you were relying too much on your presentation and not enough on God. Honestly, I prayed and prayed for the Holy Spirit's help through the whole presentation. I was utterly aware of my dependence on Him because of previous occasions of sharing and seemingly getting nowhere.

Not long after that, we had a plumber come to our house to run a new pipe. When he finished, I asked him about himself and found out that he had attended a strict religious school as a young boy. Immediately I thought that while he had heard of Jesus before, he probably didn't really understand salvation is by grace, apart from any works on our part. So I began sharing with him how Jesus had died on the cross to pay the penalty for his sins and how he could be totally forgiven as a free gift from God. Surely this must be great news for him. Nope. He looked at his watch and counted ceiling tiles as I eagerly shared with him the most important thing he could ever hear. Water off a duck's back. Finally, I paid the guy what I owed him and let him go on his way.

My fellow teammates had similar experiences. Finally, I told my teammates to forget what I had said about only spending time with people who were interested in the gospel. Nobody was! Then, we began asking the questions, "Are we missing something? If nobody is interested, what do you do? Would it be wrong to try to create interest? Is that even biblical?" I remember thinking, "Wouldn't trying to interest people in Jesus turn us into salesmen?" However, that thought didn't last long because I realized that in telling people how great Jesus is, I wouldn't have to make anything up. But trying to persuade people still felt like sales. I didn't want to start trying to play the role of the Holy Spirit. I needed to see some biblical evidence that we were actually not just supposed to present the gospel, but we should also try to get people *interested* in the gospel.

THE BIBLICAL BASIS FOR CREATING INTEREST

PAUL

Looking at the Scriptures, we quickly noticed that persuading and imploring is very much a part of the job description of an ambassador of Christ. Notice how Paul describes his ministry:

> Therefore, knowing the fear of the Lord, we *persuade* others. But what we are is known to God, and I hope it is known also to your conscience… Therefore, we are ambassadors for Christ, God making his appeal through us. We *implore* you on behalf of Christ, be reconciled to God. (2 Corinthians 5:11, 20)

Paul's ministry involved not only sharing the good news, but also trying to interest non-believers in the gospel and its implications!

PSALMS

Have you ever noticed the nature of the exhortations in the Psalms to evangelize? When the Psalmists speak of telling others about God, they speak of telling others how great he is. They tell of his faithfulness, righteousness, power, wondrous deeds, what he has done for them, and of the glory of his kingdom.

> Then my tongue shall tell of your righteousness and of your praise all the day long. (Psalm 35:28)
>
> You have multiplied, O LORD my God, your wondrous deeds and your thoughts toward us; none can compare with you! I will proclaim and tell of them, yet they are more than can be told. (Psalm 40:5)
>
> My mouth will tell of your righteous acts, of your deeds of salvation all the day, for their number is past my knowledge. (Psalm 71:15)
>
> We will not hide them from their children, but tell to the coming generation the glorious deeds of the LORD, and his might, and the wonders that he has done. (Psalm 78:4)
>
> Sing to the LORD, bless his name; tell of his salvation from day to day. (Psalm 96:2)
>
> Sing to him, sing praises to him; tell of all his wondrous works! (Psalm 105:2)
>
> And let them offer sacrifices of thanksgiving, and tell of his deeds in songs of joy! (Psalm 107:22)
>
> They shall speak of the glory of your kingdom and tell of your power... (Psalm 145:11)
>
> Psalm 18:49 says, "For this I will *praise you*, O LORD, *among the nations*, and sing to your name." Could it be that we had overlooked the need to adequately sing God's praises among the nations before we asked them to give their lives to him?

JESUS

Seeing Jesus create interest with the Samaritan woman at the well before he disclosed that he was the Messiah was the clincher for me.

JESUS SPARKED HER CURIOSITY BY ACTING DIFFERENTLY (JOHN 4:7-9)

> A woman from Samaria came to draw water. Jesus said to her, "Give me a drink." (For his disciples had gone away into the city to buy food.) The Samaritan woman said to him, "How is it that you, a Jew, ask for a drink from me, a woman of Samaria?" (For Jews have no dealings with Samaritans.)

JESUS BAITED HER WITH THE PROSPECT OF "LIVING WATER" (VV.10-12)

> Jesus answered her, "If you knew the gift of God, and who it is that is saying to you, 'Give me a drink,' you would have asked him, and he would have given you living water."
>
> The woman said to him, "Sir, you have nothing to draw water with, and the well is deep. Where do you get that living water? Are you greater than our father Jacob? He gave us the well and drank from it himself, as did his sons and his livestock."

JESUS SET THE HOOK BY TELLING OF THE AMAZING QUALITIES OF THE "LIVING WATER" (VV.13-15)

> Jesus said to her, "Everyone who drinks of this water will be thirsty again, but whoever drinks of the water that I will give him will never be thirsty again. The water that I will give him will become in him a spring of water welling up to eternal life."
>
> The woman said to him, "Sir, give me this water, so that I will not be thirsty or have to come here to draw water."

JESUS SHOWED HER THAT HER SIN WAS AN OBSTACLE TO GAINING THE "LIVING WATER" (VV.16-20)

> Jesus said to her, "Go, call your husband, and come here." The woman answered him, "I have no husband." Jesus said to her, "You are right in saying, 'I have no husband'; for you have had five husbands, and the one you now have is not your husband. What you have said is true." The woman said to him, "Sir, I perceive that you are a prophet. Our fathers

> worshiped on this mountain, but you say that in Jerusalem is the place where people ought to worship."

JESUS DEALT WITH HER QUESTIONS (VV.21-25)

> Jesus said to her, "Woman, believe me, the hour is coming when neither on this mountain nor in Jerusalem will you worship the Father. You worship what you do not know; we worship what we know, for salvation is from the Jews. But the hour is coming, and is now here, when the true worshipers will worship the Father in spirit and truth, for the Father is seeking such people to worship him. God is spirit, and those who worship him must worship in spirit and truth." The woman said to him, "I know that Messiah is coming (he who is called Christ). When he comes, he will tell us all things."

JESUS REVEALED THAT HE WAS THE SAVIOR (V.26)

> Jesus said to her, "I who speak to you am he."

Why didn't Jesus just walk up to her and say, "Hey, you are a sinner and need me. I am the Savior of the world. Repent!"? Simple: she wasn't ready for that. Jesus knew that if you share truth with someone before they really want to hear it, it will just roll off of them like "water off of a duck's back." He took time to create interest first, and because he did, she wasn't looking to leave the conversation. No, she was requesting living water from him and asking him spiritual questions. Notice the progression of her coming to faith by what she called him.

> Verse 8: "A Jew" (not a positive reference from a Samaritan)
> Verse 15: "Sir"
> Verse 19: "a prophet"
> Verse 29, 42: "The Christ" and "Savior of the world"

Jesus did evangelism differently than we had been doing it. We were just jumping in and sharing the truth before people even wanted to hear it. One of the ways I describe what we were trying to do is in terms of parking a car in a garage. We wanted to get the car (the gospel) into the garage (someone's heart), but we were failing to open the garage door (create interest) first. Let me tell you, it is not only frustrating for the driver, but it also isn't appreciated very much by the door! We began to see that evangelism involved much more than just presenting the gospel. It was a process, not an event. We needed to learn how to engage people appropriately at different stages of the process and how to help them take the next step forward. It was really freeing when we started seeing this as our role with people instead of feeling that our only objective was to get them to listen to us present the plan of salvation. It also helped us keep our focus on loving people toward Jesus instead of some task-oriented goal. So what does the process look like?

F.I.S.H.

Four simple steps of evangelism can be remembered with the acronym F.I.S.H: **F**ind, **I**nterest, **S**hare, and **H**elp. One important thing about these steps is that they are definitely sequential. One builds on another. The better job you do in a preceding step, the better job you can do with the next step. As I stated earlier, we learned that we were making the mistake of trying to share the gospel before people were even interested in hearing it.

STEP 1: FIND

This one consists of two parts: finding new people who need to hear the gospel and finding out about them.

FIND NEW PEOPLE

This one sounds easier than it is. A few years ago, my wife and I started a ministry team comprised of newly married couples. At our first meeting, I passed out 3x5 cards and asked everyone to write down ten lost people for whom they wanted to start praying so they could eventually share the gospel with them. After giving everyone a couple of minutes to think and write, I went around the room asking each person how many people they had written down. The average was two or three. We realized we couldn't move on to praying for the people on our lists and planning how we would create interest with them. Instead, we first had to figure out how we could break out of our Christian circles and meet people who didn't know the Lord. All of the other steps depend on this. Have you put yourself in a position where you are meeting a continual flow of new people? If not, the most evangelistic thing you can do in the near future may be to join a gym or a club, volunteer to tutor teens, or teach a class.

Going out and meeting new people is not easy. I personally prefer to hang out with people whom I already know well. If you are like me, I have two suggestions. First, pair up with an extrovert who just loves to meet people. Remember, Jesus sent out his disciples in teams of two (Mark 6:7; Luke 10:1). Your extroverted friend can help you meet new people, and you can help him or her be intentional with the relationships. Secondly, recognize this as an area of personal weakness and therefore an area where Christ can come shining through the most. Your obedience and dependence in this area can lead to both your increased joy and the glory of God being made known.

It is important to find a way of meeting a *continual flow of new people.* It doesn't really matter how much you know about evangelism if you don't use it. The highly effective disciple-makers we studied led twice as many people to Christ as the non-effective ones. This was not because they had more training than the others, but because they shared with twice as many people. To get those opportunities to share, you first have to meet people, lots of new people. Paul says, "The point is this: whoever sows sparingly will also reap sparingly, and whoever sows bountifully will also reap bountifully" (2 Corinthians 9:6). This principle holds true not just in giving, but in evangelism, too.

FIND OUT ABOUT PEOPLE

When we speak of finding out about people, we are talking about finding out more than just what attitude they have toward Christ. We want to find out what is going on in their lives. What real and felt needs do they have? We do this not because we view them as a project, but because we genuinely care.

The more you know about someone, the better you can create interest in the way you present the gospel to them. It is hard to help someone take the next step toward Christ if you don't know what the next step is for that person. Using a simple evangelism scale like the one below can be helpful.

ATTITUDES TOWARD CHRIST

Anti > **Open** > **Interested** > **Considering** > ✞ **(Faith)**

Through asking questions, you can learn where someone is on this scale. This will help clarify for you what the next appropriate action is with this person. If you find out the person is **Anti**, the best thing for you to do will be to pray for that person. Ask God to soften his or her heart while continuing to invest in the relationship to some degree. Sharing with someone like this could possibly harden them more. I had a fraternity brother whom I determined would just be turned off to Christ even more if I shared the gospel with him. So I prayed that God would bring some type of crisis into his life to soften him up to spiritual things. Not long after I started praying, his girlfriend broke up with him. He suddenly opened up.

If someone is **Open** but not especially interested, the next step is creating interest. If someone is **Interested**, sharing the gospel is the next step. If you have shared the gospel with a person and he or she is **Considering** following Christ, helping that person make a decision by dealing with questions and barriers is appropriate.

STEP 2: INTEREST

Around the time we were seeing the need for creating interest as a part of the evangelism process, a Thai pastor said something that seemed to fit. He said, "Thais are more affective than they are cognitive. You have to touch their hearts before you can touch their heads." That rang so true and, at the same time, was exactly the opposite of the American approach to evangelism. You see, in our western thinking, first the head must be presented with truth and adequately convinced, then the heart will be touched. Since that time, though, I have found that the best way to see Americans come to faith is not to begin by addressing their intellectual arguments, but by going for their hearts first. Once their hearts have been touched and interest has been created, most of their intellectual arguments melt away.

So how *do* you create interest? Let me tell you about a few ways.

SHOW THE RELEVANCE OF A RELATIONSHIP WITH JESUS TO CURRENT LIFE STRUGGLES

This is what Jesus did when he encountered a woman who had come out to a well looking for water. Instead of merely quenching her immediate, physical thirst, he offered her "living water" that would keep her from ever thirsting again. We can follow his example in this and show people how a relationship with Christ is what they really need.

Teaw, like most Thais, grew up in a Buddhist family. She came to Christ as a bubbly young freshman at a local college. She had an older brother named Biak. One evening she brought him to a party we were holding. Biak seemed a little uncomfortable being around a bunch of college students because he was a little older. I saw this and immediately went over and struck up a conversation with him. We had gained some clarity by this time about the importance of finding out about people before you start trying to create interest. I began asking him several questions about himself. After getting through a few basic questions about where he had studied and where he worked, I asked him if he had a girlfriend. Immediately, I knew I had struck a nerve. Biak said he had been engaged, but his fiancé had just called it off. I said,"Wow, I'm sorry about that. I'm sure it is frustrating to think you have found the right one and then, bam, it falls apart." He said, "Yeah, it is." I said, "Well, it's better to find out now instead of a couple of years into the marriage." He nodded his head in agreement. Then I said, "You know, from the number of divorces that occur and the number of couples that aren't happy after they marry, it looks like very few people marry the right person."[24] Again he nodded in agreement. I went on to say, "And the thing is, nobody stands at the altar and looks at the person he or she is marrying and thinks 'You are the wrong person.' Everyone thinks they have picked well and that they will beat the odds." Biak chimed in enthusiastically, "That's exactly right!" I said, "The only way you could be sure you are marrying the right person is to know the future or ask someone who does." Biak replied "Yeah, and nobody knows the future, right?" I answered, "Well, God knows the future and if you know him, he can help you make the right choices." Biak leaned in, stared right at me, and asked passionately, "How can I know God?" He was saying, "Sir, give me some of this living water." The look on his face and the eagerness in his voice were drastically different than the response of the plumber who was looking at his watch and counting the ceiling tiles.

Some may argue, "Isn't this approach of telling people what they will get or how they will benefit a very man-centered approach to evangelism? Shouldn't we be more God-centered by telling people that they have sinned against a holy God and that they should repent and glorify him?" Think about the invitations in Scripture to enter a relationship with Christ. All of them hold benefit for the man who responds because man is the one in need, not God. Christ promises entrance into a new kingdom, an easy yoke, eternal life, living water, an escape from punishment, fellowship with him, and on and on. Please understand that no totally depraved and unregenerate man or woman will ever come to God for noble or unselfish purposes. God is glorified in our acknowledgement that our coming to him is all about us. Jesus doesn't tell us that we can come to him without sacrifice to us, but he is quick to point out that whatever we may give up in coming to him will pale in comparison to what we will gain.[25] After regeneration (being born again), when the sanctification process begins, we should start seeing more God-centered thinking grow in believers. Pleasing him will become more and more their life aim.[26]

SHARE YOUR PERSONAL TESTIMONY

A transformed life story is powerful. Buddhists don't have a testimony about how their lives have been changed. So we began making it a habit to share how Jesus had changed our lives early on in our conversations with the lost. When we started looking at our testimonies as interest-creating tools, we realized that we needed to work on telling our stories in more compelling ways. Let me explain. Years earlier, we had all been trained to share our testimonies according to a simple three point outline. Here it is:

1. My life before Christ
2. How I came to know Jesus
3. My life since becoming a Christ follower

There is nothing wrong with this outline, but without the clear intention of telling your story in a way that creates interest, it can come out as a boring information dump. Some of us had to rework the "My life before Christ" section so that it wasn't just a list of all the sins we used to commit. We learned that it was much more interest-creating to share how we felt before we knew Christ. Those who felt helpless shared about that. Those who had no peacc learned to describe that feeling, and so on.

For many of us, the "How I came to know Christ" section contained just facts about when and where we gave our lives to Christ. We found that sharing "*Why* I decided to follow Christ" is much more interest-creating. And finally, we made some tweaks to make sure we didn't just list sins we quit doing, but actually described how Christ had changed our hearts and made a difference in our daily lives. (You can download a worksheet which will help you share your testimony in an interest-creating way at www.spiritualmultiplication.org.)

SHARE STORIES OF ANSWERED PRAYERS

God has answered a lot of my prayers over the years, and he still does. I find it extremely interest-creating to share these stories. Like the Psalmist says, "...tell of all his wondrous works!" (Psalm 105:2). I love to watch people's faces light up as I tell them the story of how, when I was a young pilot, God cleared a path for me through dark thunderstorm clouds. God did a miracle for me, and hearing about that can pique their interest.

PRAY FOR THEIR NEEDS

It was a Sunday evening right before our cell meeting. My family and two other couples had recently come together as a team to reach out to Thai professionals. While walking to our meeting, one of our team members, Melody, bumped into a surgeon who lived in our neighborhood. I'll call him Dr. P. He was out for an evening ride on his bicycle. In typical Thai fashion, he asked her where she was going. After she stumbled through trying to explain a cell meeting to a Buddhist, he asked, "Can I come?" Even though our agenda for the evening was to discuss how we might reach out to the lost in our neighborhood, Melody told him he was welcome. When Dr. P. walked in the door with Melody, I decided to change the agenda for the evening. As we all sat down, I explained that we liked to spend some of our time in each meeting getting to know each other better. I asked that we go around and each share a little about ourselves. After that, I wanted someone to give us a longer version of their life story. You see what I was doing? I was putting the ball on the tee for someone to share an interest-creating testimony. This was our *Welcome* time, the time each week where we get to know each other better.

Then we moved on to our *Witness* time. I asked if anyone would like to share how God had answered their prayers or worked in their lives since the last time we met. Again, putting the ball on the tee and aiming to create interest. After a few people shared, we moved on to our *Worship* time. We kept this rather short because we didn't want to make Dr. P. feel awkward and obligated to sing songs about a God he didn't know. We did, however, allow people to give praise and thanks to God for who he is and how he had worked in their lives. Then we moved on to our *Word* time. We read the first chapter of John, and I asked everyone to share their observations from the text and any takeaways they felt were there. Finally, we came to our *Works* time. We discussed a couple of ways we might help someone in need and then went around the room asking each person to share a prayer request. I explained to Dr. P. that we believed God always hears our prayers, and we desired to pray God's blessings on his life. I asked him if there was anything specific we could pray for him. After thinking a minute he said, "Well I have this piece of land that I have been trying to sell, and no one seems interested." We said, "Great, let's pray for it to sell." And we did.

The next Sunday evening, Dr. P. came to our meeting grinning from ear to ear. He wanted to share that he had a buyer for his land, so he wanted to attend our meeting again! At the end of the meeting, I asked Dr. P. if he would like to borrow a video I had about Jesus. He said that he would like to do so, promising to bring it back the next week. The following Sunday, he did bring it back. He said he had watched it three times! I asked him if he would like to take it again, and he said yes. A number of weeks later, Dr. P. put his faith in Christ and started bringing his wife and children to church.

LET THEM SEE CHRISTIANS INTERACTING WITH EACH OTHER IN LOVE

> By this all people will know that you are my disciples, if you have love for one another. (John 13:35)

Alm was a graduate student at Thammasat University, the Yale of Thailand. Her older sister, Onn, came to Christ through one of our staff on the college campus. Early in our ministry in Thailand, we decided that we should start having retreats to help establish young Christians in their faith. Onn turned in her registration and later asked if she could bring Alm on the retreat. We explained to Onn that this was not an evangelistic retreat and all of the teaching would be aimed at young Christians. I wasn't sure if it would be the best next step for Alm evangelistically. I have never been more wrong! It was not only the best thing for Alm, but it also helped us discover that immersing a non-Christian in the middle of a bunch of loving Christians is possibly *the* most effective interest-creating thing that can be done. You see, after the evening meeting on the first day of the retreat, Alm came to me—I guess because I was the one that just preached—and said, "Bob, I need to talk with you. There is something different here that I have never experienced. Everybody is so warm and loving. I have been on several other retreats with the university, and none of them were like this. What is going on here?" Alm's interest was through the roof. She was approaching me, asking about Christ and his power to transform lives. Alm gave her life to Christ on that retreat.

That experience with Alm was just one of the ways that the Lord was showing us that we had not been conducting our ministry according to the John 13:35 principle. That same year, we held an evangelistic retreat and had over 120 Buddhist college students attend. We invited a Thai pastor to come be the speaker. He did a great job of preaching the gospel. Showing the Jesus film appeared to move people forward, and it all seemed like a good retreat. So I was surprised by a comment the pastor made at the end. He said, "This was a good evangelistic retreat, but it would have been better if you didn't have as many lost people here." What? We poured ourselves out to get as many people as possible to come. How could fewer people hearing the gospel be better? Well, if the goal is for more people to hear the gospel, then it couldn't be better. But if the goal is for more people to be *impacted* by the gospel, then it could. Which is better, 120 attempts to park a car in the garage with five successes, or forty attempts with twenty successes? The number of Christians on this retreat was far less than the number of lost people. We were probably outnumbered four or five to one. The students who attended did not have the same experience on this retreat that Alm had on the one where the Christians were in the majority. It was not that we invited too many non-believers in an absolute sense, but we had exceeded an effective ratio of non-believers to Christians.

When we realized the power of a loving community as an interest-creating tool, we began to rethink how we did evangelism. Prior to this time, we called ourselves a team, but when it came to evangelism, our approach was really more individualistic. We would pray, play, and fellowship together. But when it came time to evangelize on campus, we would divide up and each go to our own target. Many times we would go in twos, but the overall strategy focused on penetrating a group and proclaiming the gospel. Our strategy lacked the interest-creating activity of inviting them to visit our Christian community. They didn't get to see the God-given love that we had for each other. The following diagrams contrast our initial strategy of going into their groups to tell them about Christ's love with our later strategy of bringing them into ours to *experience* his love.[27]

"Go Strategy" versus "Go *and* Bring Strategy"

We stopped just going out from a praying, playing, and fellowshipping community and started inviting lost people into *our* community. I am not simply talking about cell meetings with the five Ws (Welcome, Witness, Worship, Word, and Works), but to barbecues, parties, bowling, sports competitions, you name it! It was good for us to get into a lost group and be loving people with our new friends, but if it was just one or two of us, we could be explained away as just really nice people. On the other hand, when lost people are exposed to a whole group of people who have these qualities (love, joy, peace, forbearance, kindness, goodness, faithfulness, gentleness and self-control: the fruit of the Spirit in Galatians 5:22-23), it becomes clear that something is different. I remember inviting one of my neighbors in Birmingham to a Super Bowl party we planned for the purpose of creating interest in a few lost friends. Nobody put on a show. Everyone just acted like themselves. At the end of the party, as my neighbor was leaving, he said, "You have some *really* nice friends." He stressed "*really*" and had an almost puzzled look on his face as he said it. His garage door was opening. He had noticed something that got his attention and interested him.

After ten years in Thailand, I felt confident that the men I was leading could keep doing a great job even if I wasn't there. I had worked myself out of a job. I felt the Lord leading us back to the States to train and mobilize others to go work among the unreached. Before leaving, I did a survey of those who had come to Christ through our ministry. The survey was simple. It only had one question, "What was it that made you, a Buddhist, first consider that what the Christians were telling you might be true and worth considering?" I wanted to know what opened their garage doors. There was one tool that stood out in my survey as dominant.[28] Eighty percent told a story of how God opened them up to the gospel by letting them see the love the Christians had for one another. The love of Christ displayed in his body can be irresistible, even to some of the most resistant people on earth!

PRAY FOR GOD TO CREATE INTEREST IN THEM

If all else fails, pray. Of course I am kidding. Fervent prayer should undergird all of your interest-creating efforts. Prayer is not a step, it is the only way you will see your efforts in any of these steps bear fruit. You can't really create interest in anyone. That's a work of grace that God must do. You can plant and water, but God must make the seed of interest grow.

There will be times when nothing you are doing seems to be helping someone become interested in Christ. Times of extra prayer will be needed. I remember one specific time when it didn't seem that my Buddhist friend was growing in his interest in spiritual things at all. I got down on my knees and asked God very specifically that he would do something in my friend that week. That Saturday over lunch, he asked me if he could go to church with me! Is there someone you need to stop and pray for right now? Take a risk. Ask God for something specific!

HELP THEM SEE THEY HAVE A SIN PROBLEM

The gospel isn't good news to people who don't think they have a sin problem. I once watched the gospel roll off one of my Thai language teachers. The truth that Christ died for her sin made no impression on her at all because she felt she did not have a sin problem. Her exact words were, "I've sinned, but I'm not a sinner." You see, Buddhists only have five precepts they must obey: do not kill, steal, commit adultery, lie, or get drunk. My teacher had an incomplete law, and I had to spend time expanding her definition of sin. For example, I had to help her see that hating people was as bad as killing someone. In doing so, I was just following Jesus' example of creating interest by helping people gain an expanded understanding of sin and their need for a savior.[29] The law is a teacher that leads us to Christ by showing us our need.[30] Without it, we will not see the depths of our sin. We will be easily deceived into thinking that our good works will be enough to save us. A wise Arab believer once said, "If you want Muslims to be interested in Christ, you must make sin as high as the mountains."

We've looked at just some of the ways that interest can be created. God has used other means like suffering, healing, and dreams to open people's hearts to him. The thing for us to remember is the importance of interest-creating in the evangelism process and that it must be followed with a clear presentation of the gospel.

STEP 3: SHARE THE GOSPEL

> For I am not ashamed of the gospel, for it is the power of God for salvation to everyone who believes, to the Jew first and also to the Greek. (Romans 1:16)

Once interest has been created, it's time to share the gospel. Actually, when you are sharing how God is relevant to your daily life, how you experience his love in Christian community, how he has changed your life, how he is faithful and forgiving, and how he has answered your prayers, you *are* sharing good news. You are sharing the *gospel.* But at some point you need to pull all of the pieces together and cover some things you have not discussed before. There are a lot of good tools for this.[31]

Sometimes it is hard to tell if someone is interested in the gospel. What should you do? Without hesitation, I encourage you to go ahead and present it to them. Prayerfully, the Holy Spirit will bring interest and conviction as you share. I have seen people who have seemed disinterested give their lives to Christ. While evangelism is a process, and while it is important to create interest before presenting the gospel, I don't want you to share the gospel less often. Remember, "…whoever sows sparingly will also reap sparingly, and whoever sows bountifully will also reap bountifully" (2 Corinthians 9:6).

It is important to understand that while I am advocating creating interest before formally sharing the plan of salvation, I am not saying you should establish a friendship with someone before you communicate the gospel to them. Both the woman at the well and my Thai friend Biak became interested in the gospel within just one conversation. It was appropriate to share the gospel with them immediately.

FRIENDSHIP FIRST?

Among our survey respondents who talked with new acquaintances about "spiritual things" (not necessarily presenting a whole gospel presentation) within the first few (one to three) times they met with them, 68 percent were either effective or highly effective. In contrast, of those who waited to talk with acquaintances until after they had established an ongoing friendship, only 32 percent were effective or highly effective. Of those who mixed these approaches, 44 percent were effective or highly effective.

In the last twenty-five years, "friendship evangelism" has become increasingly popular. While the Bible plainly characterizes evangelism as a process (John 4:35-38 and 1 Corinthians 3:6), it does not teach waiting to talk about Jesus with someone until after one has developed a friendship. Only presenting the gospel to those with whom we have developed relationships will decrease the number of people we share with annually. This was found to be the case with those surveyed.

Respondents who usually share the gospel within the first few times they meet someone exposed an average of fifty-two people to the gospel annually. This average fell to fifteen for those who waited to share the gospel until they had an on-going friendship established and to twenty-five for those who employed the mixed approach. Sharing the gospel within the first few times one meets someone (and thus sharing more frequently) also resulted in more people coming to Christ. Those who shared the gospel within the first few times of meeting someone led more than 400 percent more people to Christ on average each year than those who waited to establish an ongoing relationship, and they led 44 percent more people to Christ on average each year than those who approached evangelism with a mixed approach. Don't be scared to start talking about Christ when you first meet someone. Be afraid of waiting!

STEP 4: HELP THEM MAKE A DECISION

This step involves asking for a decision and dealing with barriers. Dr. P. attended our group for weeks and heard the gospel many times and in different ways. My fellow group members started asking me, "When are you going to ask Dr. P. to make a decision for Christ?" My response was that I didn't want to rush things. He was clearly moving forward in his journey toward Christ, and I didn't want to mess it up. A few weeks later, I felt led by the Spirit to challenge him to make a clear decision to follow Christ. After one of our meetings, I said, "Dr. P., I am going to preach at church next week, and at the end of the sermon, I am going to lead people in a prayer to put their faith in Christ. I want you to consider giving your life to Christ and coming to church next week to pray that prayer." We all prayed for Dr. P. throughout the week, yet when I got up to preach, Dr. P. was not there. About three quarters of the way through the sermon, Dr. P. and his family came through the back door and sat down. After the sermon, Dr. P. came up and apologized for being late. He explained that he had to leave some medical meetings in another province and hurriedly drive three and a half hours to get to church to pray to receive Christ. I know that he had actually already come into the kingdom sometime earlier that week when he decided he would surrender his life to Christ at church. The point of the story, though, is that challenging people to make a decision for Christ is an important part of the evangelism process. You might meet someone, find out about them, create interest, share the gospel, and challenge them to make a decision for Christ all in the same day. Or it could take weeks or months. Whatever the case, realize that people benefit from being challenged to make a specific and clear decision to follow Christ.

Don't stop with "the ask," though. If they are reluctant to say yes to Jesus, find out why and address their barriers. These barriers can be theological; they may still have trouble believing that Jesus is God or that he is the only way to God. More times than not, though, the barriers are cultural, social, or moral. One of the biggest barriers for Thai college students is the fear of rejection by their parents. This was so common that I actually wrote a little booklet that addressed the issue and gave it to our staff to leave with students after they shared the gospel with them. Your job is not finished when you challenge someone to follow Christ. Satan doesn't stop then, and neither should you. Ask questions. Listen well and address their concerns. After you have addressed their concerns to the best of your ability, what should you do next? As the Spirit leads, continue to find out about them. Keep creating interest. Continue to share the gospel with them and help them by addressing the barriers to their coming to Christ (F.I.S.H.). Whatever you do, keep sowing the seed broadly with others. Otherwise, you might focus too much on people whom God will never bring to himself, missing the opportunity to share with those who would eagerly come into the kingdom.

MAKE EVANGELISM A TEAM SPORT

You can see that I believe God intends for evangelism to be a team sport. I am not talking about a golf "team" where everybody does their own thing and then adds their scores together at the end of the day. The best team sport to parallel what I am talking about is probably American football. It compares well because the players work together to advance the ball, each player does what he is good at, and there are regular huddles and a coach. When the ball crosses the goal line, it is hard to say who should get the credit. Should the quarterback who threw the ball, the receiver who caught it, the lineman who blocked, or the coach who called the play? If someone asked me how many people I led to Christ in Thailand, I would not know how to answer. Should I answer "several" or "several hundred"? It depends on how you look at it. That's the beauty of team evangelism. Nobody but God really gets the credit, and everyone on the team celebrates.

When we evangelize as a team, all the following are true:

- People can see our love for one another.
- Multiple voices add validity to the message.
- The follow-up process of integrating a new believer into community gets a huge head start, and fewer people fall away.[32]
- Believers get the leadership, structure, accountability, and teamwork they need.
- God gets the credit. As Paul wrote, "I planted, Apollos watered, but God gave the growth. So neither he who plants nor he who waters is anything, but only God who gives the growth" (1 Corinthians 3:6-7).

JUST DO IT...TOGETHER

If you asked me six weeks ago how my personal evangelism was going, I would have had to answer, "Not so hot." But if you asked me today about how it is going, I would excitedly tell you about all that has been happening over the past six weeks. What changed? I don't *know* anything more about evangelism now than I did then, so that can't be it. I didn't have a fresh mountaintop experience with the Spirit, so that can't be it either. What did happen is that a new missional community started meeting in my living room. You see, it had been a while since I was a part of a disciple-making team, and it had taken its toll on my personal evangelism, but now that is corrected.

At our first meeting, I gave everyone a 3x5 card and instructed them to write down the names of lost people with whom they wanted to share Christ. Sound familiar? I could only list two. Our homework for the week? You guessed it. Go meet someone new that we could add to our list and begin sharing Christ with them. Each week the highlight of our time together is telling what happened during the week as we shared Christ. When a new name is mentioned, it is added to a prayer poster board that we lay out on the floor in the center of the room. Just last week we were able to put a cross by one of our friend's names because he had come into the kingdom. After our sharing and prayer time for our lost friends, we move on to discussing the Word and planning evangelistic activities together.

Why do I share this with you? There are several things I would like for you to take away from my recent experience.

- Though I have led missional communities for years, have been a missionary, and can write about all that I have learned, my flesh is still weak. I don't do well living on mission without being a part of a like-minded community. I suspect you don't either.
- Ministry sharing and prayer should not be tacked on and hurried through at the end of the meeting. It is a priority and should get first billing.
- It is not rocket science. You can do it! A few 3x5 cards, a poster board, prayer, and a commitment from each member to spend at least two hours during the week with the lost (preferably along with another team member) and there you have it, the missional community you and I both need.

It is a great thing to see someone be born again, but seeing those people begin to grow in their new relationships with Christ and multiply their lives is even better. We will look in the next chapters at how highly effective disciple-makers help new believers grow, become established in their faith, and reproduce.

THE MULTIPLICATION CYCLE

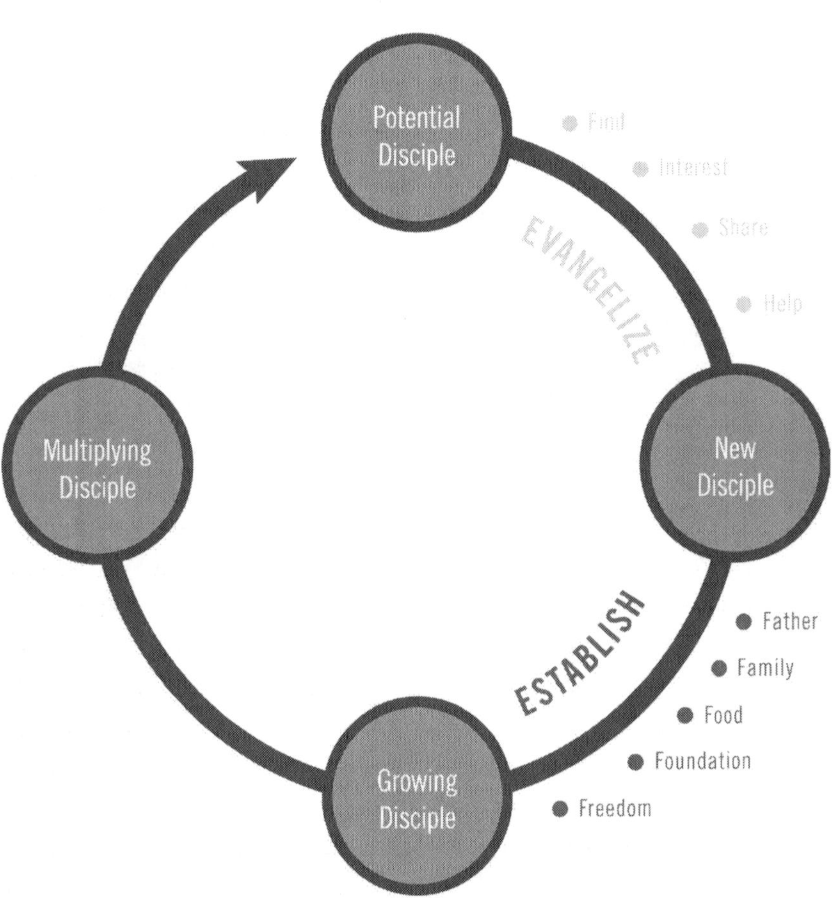

CHAPTER 7

PARENTHOOD

[ESTABLISHING]

THE NEED TO ESTABLISH NEW BELIEVERS

In the early morning hours of September 27, 1993, my wife woke me up with the news she was having contractions every ten minutes. When you live in Bangkok where babies are born in traffic jams every day, news like this gets you up out of bed and kicks your adrenal glands into high gear. Thankfully, the Lord gave me the grace to weave in and out of bumper-to-bumper Bangkok traffic like a skilled Formula One driver. Aside from some damage to my hearing from Susan's ear-piercing screams (that she swears are uncontrollable by women in labor whose husbands drive over railroad tracks at high speeds), we arrived at the hospital without incident. Then we began the long and arduous wait for the baby to arrive. Hours later, things finally picked up, and we were whisked away to the delivery room. Unfortunately, after a period of pushing, pushing, and more pushing, nothing was really happening. The doctor decided Susan needed some help, so a cadre of nurses began to hum in unison when they wanted Susan to push. They would push down on her mountain of a belly to quicken the process. Getting caught up in the moment, I even joined in with the nurses and gave a big long "huuuummmmm" along with them. I quickly learned, though, that if I valued my life, I would never "huuuummmmm" again!

Because things still weren't moving along, the doctor decided to use a suction cup on my daughter's head to pull her out. This sounded good to me at first, but I began to have second thoughts when I saw him brace himself by putting his foot on the base of the delivery table. I began to wonder, "How hard is this guy planning on pulling?" What happened next was the scariest, coolest, and grossest experience of my whole life. The doctor began to pull and nothing seemed to happen. Then he pulled harder, and I could see the veins in his arm begin to pop out. This was the scary part because

I was convinced that he was going to pull her brains out! Finally she came out, cone head and all.

I share all of this with you to ask the same question author Steve Shadrach asked, "What if I were to turn to my wife and the beaming medical staff and exude, 'Man, that was awesome! Good job, honey. Good job, everybody! That was quite an experience, but I'm sure glad it's over. Hop up, sweetheart, let's go. We've got a lot to do today, and we need to get out of here.'"[33] What if we told our new daughter, Abigail, how wonderful it was to meet her and that we hoped she had a great life and then left her? What chances would she have for survival if we abandoned her so early on? Is it any less important to provide loving and protective care to a newborn babe in Christ? Young believers are also like seedlings, which can easily be blown over and die. Those that have protection, food, and water until they are firmly *established* will have a much better chance of surviving until maturity and bearing healthy fruit.

The need for establishing new believers in the faith may be clear, but whose job is it to establish them?

WHO SHOULD WORK TO ESTABLISH NEW BELIEVERS?

If we were to examine the content of most pastors' sermons and their weekly Bible studies, we would see that most believe that the focus of their ministry should be the establishing of new believers. However, this is not what the Bible teaches. Paul told the Ephesians that church leaders are primarily to "equip the *saints*" for the ministry of establishing and maturing believers.

> And he gave the apostles, the prophets, the evangelists, the shepherds and teachers, to equip the saints for the work of ministry, for building up the body of Christ, until we all attain to the unity of the faith and of the knowledge of the Son of God, to mature manhood, to the measure of the stature of the fullness of Christ, so that we may no longer be children, tossed to and fro by the waves and carried about by every wind of doctrine… (Ephesians 4:11-14)

As we start to unpack the method of establishing someone in the faith, we will see that it is impossible for one person in a church to succeed at such an intensive work alone. With most pastors today focused on establishing instead of their biblically assigned role of equipping the saints to disciple others, is it any wonder that few churches produce multiplying disciples? Are we surprised that so many pastors burn out? Wouldn't it be great if every pastor had a trained army of equipped saints to share the workload? According to Ephesians, that is exactly God's intention for every church!

DEFINITION OF ESTABLISHING

Gaining a clear understanding of what it means to establish someone in the faith will help you stay focused as you engage in this important phase of ministry. Since establishing is just one part of the larger job of discipling, let's look at a definition of discipling first. In his helpful book *Discipleship,* Allen Hadidian defines discipling this way:

> Discipling others is the process by which a Christian with a life worth emulating commits himself for an extended period of time to a few individuals who have been won to Christ, the purpose being *to aid and guide their growth to maturity* and equip them to reproduce themselves in a third spiritual generation.[34] *[emphasis added]*

The work of establishing is seen in the words "to aid and guide their growth to maturity." While this is the best definition of discipling I have heard, we must add one thing to it: *the integration of new believers into the life of a disciple-making team.* The new definition would read like this:

> Discipling others is the process by which a Christian with a life worth emulating commits himself for an extended period of time to a few individuals who have been won to Christ, the purpose being to aid and guide their growth to maturity *and integration into the life of a disciple-making team* for their equipping to reproduce themselves in a third spiritual generation.

This is important because helping a new Christian become established in the faith does not mean moving him or her from dependence on you to independence. No Christian is meant to live the Christian life independently of other believers. *Inter*dependence, rather, is the goal. It would be hard to imagine a firmly established or reproducing believer who was not deeply involved in a disciple-making body.

Besides being integrated into a faith family, a new believer also needs a spiritual father (or mother), grounding in the foundations of the faith, the ability to feed on God's Word, and freedom from bondages to sin. With these things in mind, let us move on to examine how these five things not only define an established believer but also serve as growth multipliers.

GROWTH MULTIPLIERS

When I first started learning to speak the Thai language, my teacher taught me a couple of "power questions" that served to multiply my language learning. With these questions, I could learn Thai not just when I was with her but wherever I went in Thailand. Learning to ask *"Nee, riak waa aray krap?"* ("What do you call this?") enabled me to learn any noun to which I could point. Learning to ask *"Pom kamlang tom aray?"* ("What am I doing?") enabled me to learn any verb I could act out. In the same way, there are certain growth multipliers in the Christian life that can greatly accelerate the growth of new believers.

GROWTH MULTIPLIER ONE: A SPIRITUAL FATHER OR MOTHER

It is undisputed that those baby Christians who have a spiritual father or mother—a mature believer who sticks around and fulfills the God-given nurturing role—will grow much faster than spiritual orphans. The apostle Paul clearly saw himself as having the responsibility of a father to those whom he led to Christ: "For though you have countless guides in Christ, you do not have many fathers. For I became your father in Christ Jesus through the gospel" (1 Corinthians 4:15-17).

Over 80 percent of believers we surveyed who had never been discipled fell into the category of non-effective disciple-makers. This number decreased to 50 percent for those who had been discipled. Clearly, having a spiritual mentor makes a difference not only in one's own personal growth, but also in the likelihood of spiritual reproduction. Effective and highly effective disciple-makers tended to have been discipled for longer than non-effective disciple-makers. Remember that only 12 percent of those surveyed scored as highly effective. However, this number rose to 30 percent for those who had been discipled between 2.5-3.5 years. Looks like Jesus knew what he was doing when he spent about three years with his disciples!

While these numbers clearly imply the benefits of longer discipling relationships, we found the data also left no room for doubting the importance of quality in the discipling relationship. Beyond asking the survey participants how long they were discipled, we asked them to rate how helpful those relationships had been. There is a strong correlation between the helpfulness of that relationship and effectiveness in disciple-making. Quality was more important than quantity. Disengaged and half-hearted parenting isn't any more likely to produce star performance in spiritual children than it is in physical children.

Dawson Trotman, founder of the Navigators, a ministry focused on multiplying disciples, used to ask people "Where's your man?" or "Where's your woman?" That's a great question for us to use to see if we are multiplying others. I'm afraid that most Christians wouldn't be able to point to their people. Would you? Now that disciple-making is a bit more popular, and more people are at least claiming to be taking part, we need to ask the quality question. Would your disciples say you are very present in their lives and helpful to their growth and ministry? Mark says that Jesus appointed twelve "so that they might *be with him* and he might send them out to preach."[35] Would your disciples say they are frequently "with you," or are you an absent parent?

While being present is important, it is no guarantee of being helpful. Let's pause here and ask the question, "What are the most helpful activities in which a spiritual parent can engage?"

PARENTING ACTIVITY: PRAYER

The apostle Paul spoke frequently of how he got on his knees to pray for new believers.[36] I will never forget the many times I barged into the dorm room of Jay, one of the men who discipled me, and found him down on his knees praying for me. Joel Comiskey found that cell group leaders who prayed more for the people in their groups saw their groups multiply more frequently.[37] We see Jesus being a protective parent by praying for Peter and his faith.

> Simon, Simon, behold, Satan demanded to have you, that he might sift you like wheat, but I have prayed for you that your faith may not fail. And when you have turned again, strengthen your brothers. (Luke 22:31-32)

Praying for your spiritual children is not optional, it's essential! If you want to see your spiritual children multiply, it is going to take time invested on your knees. What should you pray about to help your disciples? I would suggest using *The Multiplication Cycle* diagram presented at the beginning of this section. Pray them around the cycle. If they are "New Disciples" who need establishing to become "Growing Disciples," then I would pray for growth in the five "**F**s":

- **F**ather: Pray about their relationship with you.
- **F**amily: Pray they will bond with other believers and integrate into the family of God.
- **F**ood: Pray they will learn to self-feed on God's Word daily.
- **F**oundations: Pray they will grow strong and deep in their knowledge of God and the doctrines of the faith.
- **F**reedom: Pray they will grasp their position in Christ and experience the freedom that is theirs in him.

PARENTING ACTIVITY: ENCOURAGING

When Peter was about to come under spiritual attack, Jesus didn't just pray for him. He very intentionally spoke words to him that would encourage and empower him at what must have been the low point of his life. Let's look at the Luke 22 passage again:

> "Simon, Simon, behold, Satan demanded to have you, that he might sift you like wheat, but I have prayed for you that your faith may not fail. And when you have turned again, strengthen your brothers." (Luke 22:31-32)

When I put myself in Peter's sandals, I can't imagine continuing to minister to others after I had blown it by failing my Savior and friend, not once, but three times. Jesus knew that Peter would feel utterly disqualified after he denied him three times, so he proactively gave him the encouragement and empowerment he would need. Jesus told him that after he had failed, he was to turn back to God and then get back into ministering to others ("strengthen your brothers"). Jesus shows us that great spiritual fathers are constant encouragers and believe in their kids even when they don't believe in themselves.

True encouragement comes from God himself. The Greek word *parakaleo* is often translated "encourage" in our English Bibles. *Parakaleo* literally means "to call near" and is used in the Bible in the context of one's relationship with God. Think of the prefix para. We use it in words like "para-medic" or "para-church" to mean alongside. Since encouraging someone means calling them close to God, you must be near to God first if you want to call others to him.

What do you do if you don't feel like you are close to God? Admit it to those you disciple and ask if they will pursue God with you. As you all move closer to God together, everyone's level of courage will rise.

How you encourage others will need to vary because not everyone connects with God in the same way. Gary Thomas correctly points out that each of us has a primary pathway to God.[38] While venturing out into nature and having some time alone with God really fills me, it doesn't seem to encourage my wife in the same way. Her pathway is more intellectually-oriented. So, when I think about encouraging her, I don't ask her to strap on her hiking boots. She is ministered to most when I serve her by simply removing something from her to-do list so she can have some time alone with God to think things through and reflect on him. Great leaders learn how each of their disciples draws near to God and finds ways to help them do it.

PARENTING ACTIVITY: TEACHING

Teaching turbocharges our disciples' growth when we focus on three things: discovery, obedience, and transference.

Discovery

What do you think of when you imagine yourself teaching the people you disciple? Does the mental picture include you and your disciples sitting around a table or on sofas with Bibles open and you doing the talking? I hope not. Certainly, there are times when something like that will be appropriate, but for the most part, that method of teaching won't produce a lot of results. People understand and retain things best when they discover them for themselves. Good teachers (like Jesus) impact people deeply by asking great questions.

Obedience

Hopefully, your disciples are getting a good sermon each week from attending a solid local church. Rather than giving them a second sermon when you meet, why not ask some guiding questions to facilitate discussion about how to *apply* what was taught in the sermon? Unfortunately, most of us default to shoving more knowledge into our disciples' brains when they aren't even applying what they have already heard. We misunderstand the command Jesus gave us and therefore miss out on building a real growth multiplier into the lives of those we disciple. Take a close look at our commission to make disciples:

> Go therefore and make disciples of all nations, baptizing them in the name of the Father and of the Son and of the Holy Spirit, teaching them to observe all that I have commanded you. And behold, I am with you always, to the end of the age. (Matthew 28:19-20)

Did Jesus tell us to make disciples by teaching them all that he taught? No. What are we to teach them? *Obedience* to all of his commands. Certainly you can't obey what you don't know, but learning the commands is the easy part. Consistently obeying the commands in our daily lives is the difficult part. This practice of teaching disciples to *obey* the Word through discussing application then holding each other accountable to living it out is at the center of every wildly multiplying church planting movement today.[39] If you have discipled someone in the past or are doing so right now, ask yourself the question, "What has been my focus: content or obedience?" Can you see how teaching someone to obey would be a growth multiplier? My job as a parent with my three daughters is not to teach them all of the laws of the land, the rules at school, policies of future employers, and all the commands of God. My focus rather needs to be on teaching them to obey and how to do it with the right heart attitude.

Transference

We all desire that what we teach our disciples would sink in and become their own. Getting them to share what they are learning with others as quickly and frequently as possible is the key. For this to happen, though, they may need permission and vision from you to do so. They need you to empower them for action.

Many new believers feel very inadequate to share anything spiritual with someone else. They fear that they don't know the Bible well enough or haven't been a Christian long enough to answer questions with any authority. They need you to tell them it is okay for them to share with others even if they can't answer all the questions they might be asked.

Nothing straps a rocket onto the back of a new believer like vision. A part of the empowering process is to share Scriptures that point to God's desire to use his children in great ways to impact eternity. Empowering young believers to action will serve to accelerate their spiritual growth and solidify their new beliefs. Challenge them to pass along what they are learning from you every single week!

Of course, the starting point for me teaching them is to set the example for them in my own obedience and the attitudes of my heart. It starts with me modeling it.

PARENTING ACTIVITY: MODELING

The axiom, "More is caught than taught," is as true today as it was two thousand years ago when Jesus modeled life and ministry for his disciples. We are fooling ourselves if we think we are going to produce mature and multiplying disciples by meeting once a week over coffee or in a small group. There is no impact without contact. Weekly hit-and-runs won't get the job done. Think about it. Who are the top two people who have impacted your life? Was it what they sat down and taught you, or *who they were* that most impacted you? It's almost always the latter. Jesus knew what he was doing when he chose twelve to "be with him." Teaching is important, but it must be done in the context of modeling to be best understood and reproduced.

How are we to do this in the real world with a job and family? You fight for it! You make a series of intentional decisions to make it happen. You are intentional with whom you eat your breakfasts and lunches. You try not to run errands or watch a football game alone. You invite your disciples to go with you to your daughter's soccer game. You invite singles to live in your home. (My wife and I bought a house with a basement so that a couple guys I'm discipling can live with us.) You help your disciples paint their homes and get them to help you paint yours. You don't do evangelism alone. Spend time each week doing some sort of evangelism *together*.

I saw my own need for models in my life when it came to growing in the area of encouraging others. It's not something that comes naturally to me. In fact, it was a weakness of mine for many years. One of my first ministry leaders pointed this out. I did all kinds of Bible studies about encouraging others, and that helped some, but to be honest, I didn't get much better until several years later. I came under the leadership of a different man, and I was able to see a real encourager in action. Guess what happened. I finally started to show some noticeable growth in this area! My first leader was correct in what he said, but encouraging others wasn't a real strength of his either. The real growth came in my life when I *saw* someone live out the verses I had studied.

In his letter to the Corinthians, Paul affirmed the truth that we become like the people with whom we spend our time. Notice how he didn't just expect his example to impact his spiritual son Timothy, but he expected the impact to have a ripple effect into the lives of others. See how when Paul wanted the Corinthians to imitate him, he sent them Timothy!

> For though you have countless guides in Christ, you do not have many fathers. For I became your father in Christ Jesus through the gospel. I urge you, then, be *imitators* of me. *That is why I sent you Timothy*, my beloved and faithful child in the Lord, to remind you of my ways in Christ, as I teach them everywhere in every church. (1 Corinthians 4:16-17)

While having a spiritual father or mother is a tremendous growth multiplier, these verses show us that disciple-making is a team effort. This brings us to a powerful growth multiplier: Family.

GROWTH MULTIPLIER TWO: FAMILY

My third daughter, Ashley, is a remarkable young lady. Skilled in so many areas, she knows and can do all kinds of things that I never taught her. Sometimes I ask myself, "Where did she learn how to do all this stuff?" The answer is really not that hard. She learned it from her sisters and her mom. If I were the only prayer warrior, encourager, teacher, and model in her life, she would not nearly be the young lady that she is today. The same is true with spiritual children. God doesn't just want new Christians to have spiritual parents. He wants them to have close and meaningful relationships with several other brothers and sisters in Christ.

I believe that when Jesus instructs us to baptize people as a part of the disciple-making process, he isn't simply referring to immersing them in water. He wants them connected into a family of believers who will love and nurture them as one of their own. Can you see why I call this a growth multiplier? One-on-one discipling does not speed up someone's spiritual growth but actually keeps it from accelerating. Deep fellowship and ministry teamwork with multiple brothers or sisters in Christ will naturally help someone grow faster than just being with one other individual. Sure, some occasional one-on-one time can be helpful and is always a part of the life-on-life discipling process, but getting young believers integrated into a small family of believers should always be top priority. If one positive influence in a young believer's life is good, several is even better. Notice how Paul shared the role and responsibilities of spiritual parenthood with those on his disciple-making team:

> For you know how, like a father with his children, *we* exhorted each one of you and encouraged you and charged you to walk in a manner worthy of God, who calls you into his own kingdom and glory. (1 Thessalonians 2:11-12)

Jesus didn't disciple people one-on-one. Individual disciples don't do well when they are not a part of a disciple-making team. Our research showed that the most effective disciple-makers were those who led small groups of between five and twelve people. These disciple-makers also selected three to four people to specifically focus on. Does this sound familiar? Jesus intentionally built twelve men into a team and family. Out of that group, he focused even more attention on three men: Peter, James, and John. Disciple-makers who want to see their vision of multiplication take place in the real world would be wise to follow this example. The old acronym for TEAM—**T**ogether **E**veryone **A**ccomplishes **M**ore—is certainly true when it comes to spiritual growth and ministry!

GROWTH MULTIPLIER THREE: FOOD

"Like newborn babies, long for the pure milk of the word, so that by it you may grow in respect to salvation" (1 Peter 2:2 NASB). Without food, no baby grows. Without the spiritual food of the Word, no child of God will grow either. How healthy do you think you would be if you only ate once or twice a week? Unfortunately, most Christians only feed on the Word once a week when their pastors spoon-feed them. Some will get one more meal each week when their small group or discipleship leader feeds them. But this still gives them only two meals. Who could live on that? What if we taught those whom we are discipling how to feed themselves? What kind of multiplying effect would that have on their growth? This seems like a no-brainer, doesn't it? Teaching people to self-feed is something every laborer for Christ should understand and focus on, right? Unfortunately, the focus of most disciplers seems to be on feeding those they lead instead of teaching them to feed themselves.

I recently had a free hour between appointments at a local university. I sat in the food court and started catching up on e-mail. At the table next to me were two young ladies. The older one had an open Bible in front of her. For the next forty-five minutes, I heard her masterfully teach a lesson to the younger one. I'm sure the younger girl walked away knowing more than she did when they began, but I had to wonder how many more meals she would get from the Word that week. Could a knowledge-based lesson like that really result in much life change without some extended reflection on the truths just piled on her? Probably not.

For people to become self-feeders, you will want to help them develop in three areas relating to God's word: conviction, competence, and consistency.

CONVICTION

Disciples who have a conviction that feeding on God's Word is important desire to do so on a regular basis. They will grow in this conviction as they observe it taught in God's Word, see it modeled in your life, and experience the practical benefits from it in their own lives. When people self-feed, they learn through discovery. Truths found in God's Word through their own digging usually impact them more deeply than those they are spoon-fed. This impact and the thrill of finding treasures in

God's Word themselves deepens their conviction that they must feed on it more regularly!

COMPETENCE

Disciples who are competent self-feeders know how to take in God's Word in such a way that it brings significant nourishment to their souls, direction for their lives, and changes in their way of thinking. They can draw appropriate applications to their context, and their obedience brings life change. Feeding on God's Word involves more than just taking it in through reading. When we had our first child, I learned that just getting food into the mouth doesn't mean it will be digested and provide nourishment. My wife began introducing solid food like peas and carrots to our daughter Abigail before she had a full set of working teeth. I helped with the task of changing diapers. One evening, things were smelling pretty bad, so I took Abigail into the bedroom for a diaper change. Do you know what I saw in her diaper? Peas and carrots! I burst out of the bedroom looking for Susan to tell her that until Abigail grew more teeth, she needed to mash up the peas and carrots for her or else Abigail would not get any nourishment from them. As you can see, input is no guarantee of nourishment.

As a young Christian, I was introduced to the hand illustration seen below used by the Navigators.[40]

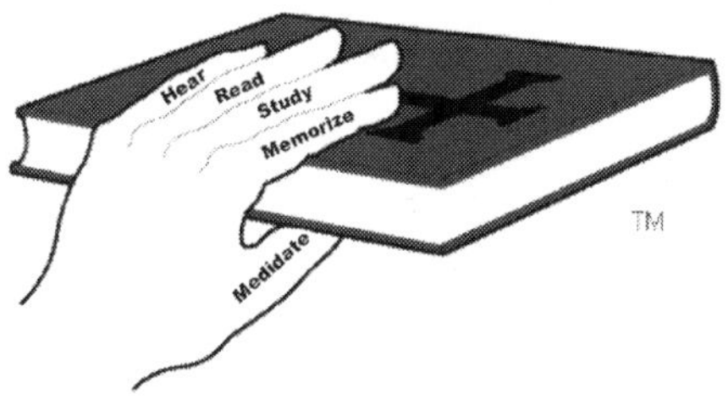

This graphic illustrates five different means of interacting with the Word. One important point of the illustration is that meditation needs to be coupled with all of the other means of interaction. If you held a Bible in your hand and then took your thumb away, the Bible would fall. Undigested peas and carrots go right through a baby without providing any nourishment. Likewise, hearing, reading, studying, and memorizing the Word without meditating on it for the sake of application will also provide little benefit to the believer. Lots of exposure to the Word is no guarantee that growth will take place. Notice how the believers mentioned in the book of Hebrews fell into this trap of being overexposed and underdeveloped:

> For though by this time you ought to be teachers, you need someone to teach you again the basic principles of the oracles of God. You need milk, not solid food... (Hebrews 5:12)

One of the great dangers of intake without meditation is that you may very easily become puffed up.[41] Help the people you are discipling avoid this trap by becoming competent in digesting God's Word. To accomplish this, you will need to help them with the skills of observation, interpretation, and application. Before I go on, let me mention one potential pitfall about training them in these things. I have had the privilege of receiving very extensive training in Bible study skills and interpretation. Over the years I have trained others in these same skills, only to notice later that neither they nor I were using even 20 percent of what we had learned on a regular basis. My approach now is to keep things very simple. Strive for consistent usage of simple tools. Along with these tools, I always take the time to cover some very important principles of Bible interpretation.

One of the most helpful self-feeding tools I have used over the years is a list of questions that aid in meditation for life change. You can find them in Appendix 2. These are the teeth that will help you and your disciples chew on God's Word and get the maximum nourishment from it. Besides using these questions, I want to share one secret that will make your and your disciples' time in the Word 75 percent more fruitful. I'm not kidding. It is really that helpful! *Use a pen and paper to write down all your observations, interpretations, and applications.* The quality of your time alone with God in his Word will be noticeably better than when you don't write anything down. When the quality of your time in God's Word goes up, so does your enjoyment of it. This is extremely important to help with the next area: consistency.

CONSISTENCY

It is not enough to see something as important (conviction) and know how to do it (competency). If it were, most of the people who are overweight due to laziness (not some medical reason) would get up off their sofas and walk thirty minutes a day. Remember, conviction plus competence does not necessarily equal consistency. Our best chance at consistency comes when community is combined with conviction and competence. If your disciples (or you) are having trouble getting consistent time alone with God, by all means, start meeting together to do it. After a while, they will start to love their time with God and not need your presence as much.

Consistency also comes much more easily when we enjoy and benefit from an activity. There is a state park less than a mile from my house. Just about every weekend, the bike trails are full of adventurous bikers. Few of the guys I know who ride there have accountability partners to make sure they ride. They do it because they love it.

Sometimes, when people are not consistent in getting alone with God, it is because they don't get much out of it when they do. If you or those whom you disciple aren't enjoying time alone with God, it is not because God is not enjoyable to be with. It is because you or they have not truly learned how to interact with him in a meaningful way. If you think this might be the reason your disciples are struggling with being consistent in personal devotions, spend time helping them grow in their competence. If you are struggling with this, seek out the help of a respected mentor, and be honest about your struggle. Regular and sweet fellowship with the Lord is foundational to all of life and ministry. We should never settle for a lack of desire for him.

> For a day in your courts is better than a thousand elsewhere. I would rather be a doorkeeper in the house of my God than dwell in the tents of wickedness. (Psalm 84:10)

Along with a consistent pattern of feeding on God's Word, it is important to establish a habit of locking in those truths through Scripture memory. Besides meditation, Scripture memory is probably the greatest turbo charger for Christian growth. Surprisingly, when I recently surveyed a group of full-time Christian workers, I found that over half were *not* consistently memorizing the Word. How about you and your disciples? Could this be an easy area to improve and thus see some real growth occur in your lives? Feeding on and retaining God's Word nourishes our souls and helps us build deep foundations in our lives.

GROWTH MULTIPLIER FOUR: FOUNDATIONS

My wife and I lived amid the skyscrapers of Bangkok for eight years. While we were there, it seemed like the skyline was always decorated with cranes building even more and taller towers. What was so inspiring to me, though, was not how tall these buildings stretched upward, but how far the builders would dig down to lay their foundations. The taller the tower, the deeper the foundation. It always seemed like it would take forever to see the building grow out of the hole they were working in. Once the foundation was finished, though, it was incredible to see how fast the building would grow into the sky.

FOUNDATIONS FIRST

Christians whose growth never seems to take off are most likely suffering from faulty foundations. Remember how the writer of Hebrews scolded his readers for not growing, urging them to start practicing what they had learned so they could move on to more advanced teachings. Without a solid foundation, they would have to continue going over the basics. His exhortations to them give us at least a partial list of the foundations of the Christian life:

> Therefore, let us leave the elementary doctrine of Christ and go on to maturity, not laying again a foundation of repentance from dead works and of faith toward God, and of instruction about washings, the laying on of hands, the resurrection of the dead, and eternal judgment. (Hebrews 6:1-2)

From this passage and others like it, I suggest the following as a list of foundational teachings for disciple-makers to work through with those they disciple[42]:

- The gospel (doctrine) of Christ and his kingdom
- The proper response to the gospel—repentance and faith
- The practice of Christ's Lordship in our daily lives ("teaching them to obey")
- The meaning and importance of water baptism and immersion into the body of Christ
- The Spirit-filled life ("the laying on of hands")

- The doctrine of eternal judgment, the resurrection from the dead, and the implications for mission
- The believer's position in Christ and assurance of salvation
- A biblical perspective on suffering
- How to spend time with God in the Word and prayer (including the value of Scripture memory)
- Spiritual warfare

TEACHING FOUNDATIONS THROUGH USING MATERIALS

In discussions of how to teach the foundations of the faith, the question of whether or not to use a fixed set of discipleship materials often arises. I am a teacher, and I like to develop or select tools as I go that seem to meet the specific needs of those I disciple. Others just prefer to buy something off the shelf and stick with it. Over the years, I have engaged in hundreds of conversations with disciple-makers about the pros and cons of having a fixed set of materials. One side of the argument stresses flexibility and tailoring the approach to the individual, while the other side espouses the value of sticking to one set of materials for the sake of reproducibility. I have argued for both sides over the years. Which side is right? The following chart displays our research findings.

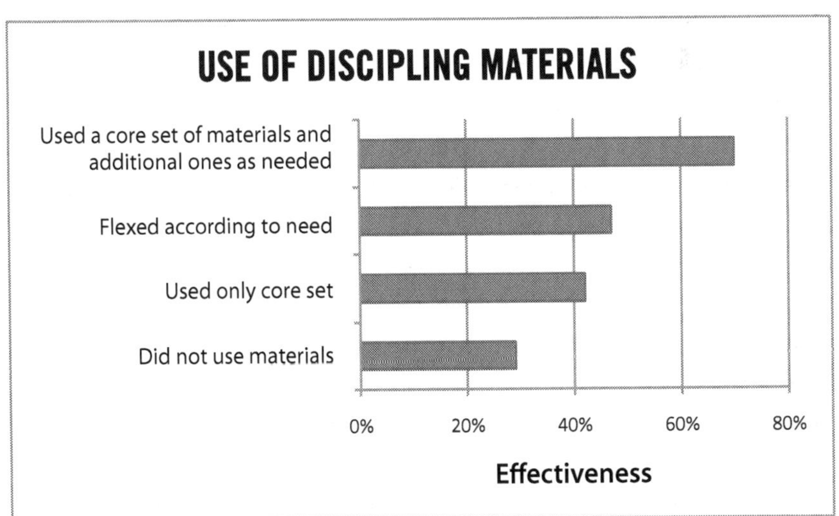

Bottom line: using a core set of materials with limited additional tools as needed proved to be the best approach. In this day and age, we tend to think that anything that is customized must be better, right? Apparently, when it comes to *establishing* disciples, too much customization is not a good thing. Why is this?

The basic needs of new disciples are the same.

The foundations of the faith do not differ from one disciple to another. By necessity, foundations must be laid first. It would be a mistake to skip over the basics in an attempt to tailor a curriculum to meet your disciples' felt needs or interests. Just because they are interested in studying eschatology in the book of Revelation doesn't mean that's where you should start with them. It's a pretty sure bet that studying things like the gospel and assurance of salvation would better lay a foundation for their spiritual future.

Simplicity aids confidence and reproducibility.

One of the most solidifying things for one's faith is to teach it to someone else. Empowering new disciples to start discipling others quickly will be tremendously helpful to their growth. Most likely, though, they will not be discerning of what is foundational and what is superstructure. Whatever you did with them is what they will turn around and attempt to do with someone else. If you take me through "Book 1," there is a good chance I will feel like I can take someone else through Book 1. If you pull a little from here and a little from there and customize things to "my needs," there is a good chance that I will be impressed with your knowledge and insight and feel that there is no way I could do that for someone else. Reproduction happens more frequently when we give people clear tracks to run on.

A new disciple's integration into the family is more important than getting a perfectly customized curriculum in a one-on-one setting.

We as disciple-makers must see our personal limitations and do everything we can to help new believers develop meaningful friendships with other believers. The book of Proverbs speaks of the benefit of having a plurality of counselors.[43] Get your disciples into community early on to maximize their protection and growth.

Keeping the focus on outreach is crucial.

When the focus of a relationship or small group becomes the growth of those in it, their growth is actually stunted. An emphasis on customizing curriculum to meet the needs of those in a group can subtly lead it away from a missional focus. You will lose all of the beneficial issues that being on mission raises.

So all customization is bad? Not at all. It is a matter of timing. While customizing should be kept to a minimum during the *Establishing* stage, it becomes pretty important in the *Equipping* stage where the needs of individual disciples diverge.

Since using good materials has proven important, I have attempted to write a simple and easily transferable set. It is built from the ground up on all of the principles and research discussed in this book. These materials are not just written to increase knowledge but to guide the disciple into living within a multiplying missional community. My prayer is that they will help you and your disciples do exactly that. You can find these resources at www.spiritualmultiplication.org.

TEACHING FOUNDATIONS THROUGH LIFE-ON-LIFE DISCIPLING

While materials can be helpful tools, we must always remember that only life-on-life missional discipleship will produce well-rounded and mature disciples. Anyone who has ever heard of disciple-making has no doubt also heard what Paul wrote to Timothy: "and what you have heard from me in the presence of many witnesses entrust to faithful men who will be able to teach others also" (2 Timothy 2:2). Paul obviously had some curriculum which he taught publically and which he wanted Timothy in turn to pass on to others. But it would be a huge mistake to think these teaching points were all that Timothy learned from Paul. No, Paul reviews for Timothy what he had learned from him in 2 Timothy 3:10-11:

> You, however, have followed my teaching, my conduct, my aim in life, my faith, my patience, my love, my steadfastness, my persecutions and sufferings that happened to me at Antioch, at Iconium, and at Lystra—which persecutions I endured; yet from them all the Lord rescued me.

Other than Paul's teaching, which of the things he lists above would Timothy have primarily learned from listening to him teach?

- His conduct? No.
- His aim in life? Nope.
- His faith? Only partially.
- His patience, love, or steadfastness? Not a chance.

How did Timothy learn these? By being "with him" as he ministered in Antioch, Iconium, and Lystra and watching how Paul endured even though he was persecuted in those places. There is an even bigger lesson that Timothy learned from Paul. To see it, we will have to review what happened to Paul and his companions in each of those locations.

- Antioch – The Jews stirred up people against them, but they left unharmed.[44]
- Iconium – They learned of a plot to harm them so they fled.[45]
- Lystra – Paul was stoned so badly that the attackers assumed he was dead.[46]

Now what attitude did Paul have about these events? "...yet from them all the Lord rescued me" (2 Timothy 3:11). Wait a minute. They nearly stoned Paul to death at Lystra, and Timothy watched it. So how can Paul say to Timothy, "...yet from them all the Lord rescued me"? Timothy knew that the Lord didn't rescue Paul from the stoning at Lystra. Paul could say this because Timothy had watched Paul live out a belief and attitude that sometimes the Lord delivers you from having to experience a problem, and sometimes the Lord delivers you *through* the endurance of the problem. No doubt Timothy's systematic theology textbook had flesh on it, and the important parts were underlined with bruises and scars. While using discipling materials to establish new believers in the foundations of the faith is helpful, we must never rely on them apart from a life-on-life discipling relationship.

GROWTH MULTIPLIER FIVE: FREEDOM

In the early 1990s in Bangkok, our campus ministry and church planting team held weekly staff meetings to pray for the ministry, discuss how things were going, and plan for the coming week. For a number of weeks, we had been discussing how a lot of the new Christians seemed to be tangled up with all sorts of problems. Our staff would counsel them, but it seemed like week after week they would just return to their small group and continually vent about their problems (family discord, romantic heartbreaks, friendship drama, financial difficulties…) without making any progress. Eventually, one of our staff members suggested we just shut the church down and start over with new people who didn't have so many problems. After considering that idea briefly through a mixture of laughter and tears, we decided that a new group of people would probably have a lot of the same problems that this group had. We stuck with the group and prayed for answers.

Not long after that, one of our staff members found some videos that explained how disciplers need to help people find freedom in Christ before they can see them make significant strides forward in their spiritual growth. It made perfect sense to us! We had been trying to propel people forward who seemed to have a ball and chain around their ankles. Nobody was getting anywhere! We began reading and studying the Scriptures to learn more about spiritual bondages and how to help people find freedom in Christ. Then we began taking those whom we were personally discipling through the Scriptures to show them that, in Christ, they were not only free from the penalty of sin, but they were also free from the power of sin. Verses like, "So if the Son sets you free, you will be free indeed" (John 8:36) began to come alive and have real meaning. We started seeing some dramatic changes in people's lives, and we were finally able to see people move forward in the discipleship process. Someone who is in an endless sin-confess-sin-confess cycle is never going to make real progress in growth and ministry. Bondages must be broken.

Bondages in a Christian's life can come in many forms. For some, the bondage is bitterness, the inability to forgive. For others, it is wrong thoughts and depression. For many, it involves alcohol or drugs. The most common addiction for men is that of pornography. All of your disciples will have some level of bondage in their lives. You will not be able to see them make real progress in their spiritual growth until they deal with it and gain a significant level of freedom. Be encouraged, though, and know that I have personally seen dozens of people come to experience a degree of liberty that they never thought would be possible.[47]

SUMMARY

New believers need spiritual parents who establish them in the faith by providing the growth multipliers of a Father, a Family, Food, Foundations, and Freedom. Remember that the goal of parenting is to work yourself out of a job. Don't allow them to be an only child. Get them integrated into the family. Don't just feed them; teach them to self-feed. Don't answer questions; show them how to find answers in God's Word. As Howard Hendricks says, "Don't ever do anything for your kids that they can do for themselves." As you do this, your spiritual children will grow into adults and have children of their own, and you will have great joy like the apostle John: "I have no greater joy than to hear that my children are walking in the truth" (3 John 1:4). It's a privilege to help disciples become established in their faith, but it's an even greater joy to see them become equipped to minister and reproduce. The next chapter will unpack how to go beyond just making disciples to making disciple-makers!

THE MULTIPLICATION CYCLE

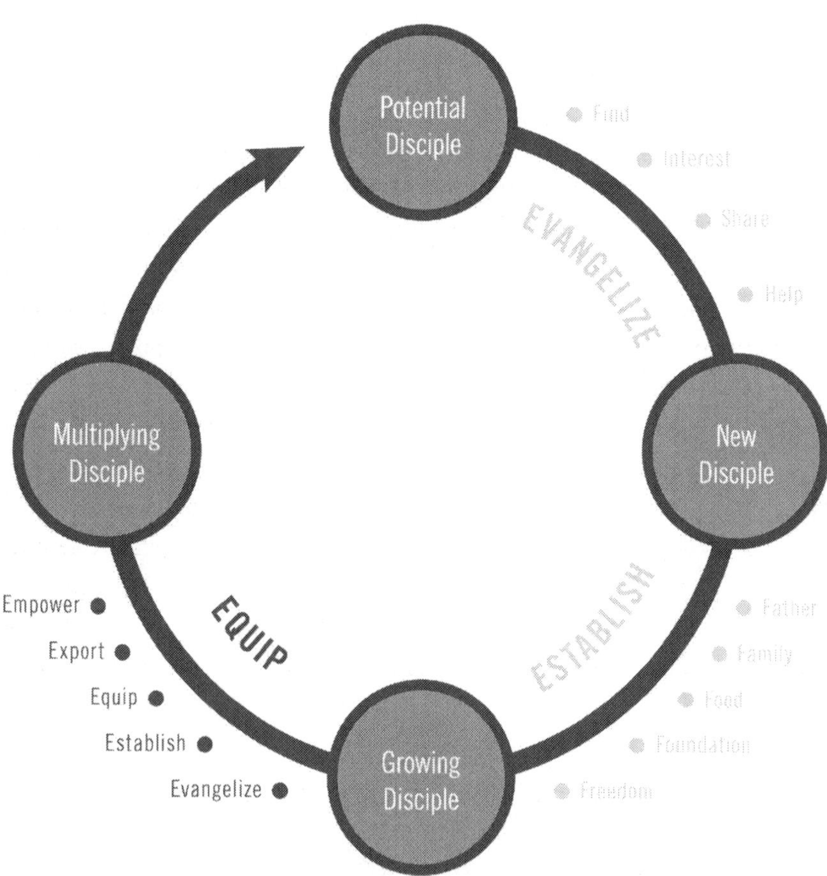

CHAPTER 8

LEARNING TO FLY

[EQUIPPING]

Is our goal to make disciples or make disciple-makers? When Jesus finished his training of the twelve, he told them to "make disciples." He had not just evangelized and established them; he had equipped them to repeat the process with others. Unfortunately, most of today's discipling efforts end once disciples are established. One of the reasons this occurs is that people don't really comprehend the equipping process. Equipping is developing people in their character and ministry skills so they can effectively evangelize, establish, equip, export, and empower others to do the same. Misunderstandings about how equipping is done, the focus of equipping, whom should be equipped, and the context and duration of the process often lead to a failure to multiply. In this chapter, we'll look at the equipping ministry of Jesus to help us grasp and demystify this important discipleship stage. The need to do so is critical because most discipling materials focus on establishing, which gets us studying, not doing. The result is people who know a lot but do little. The missing secret sauce is on-the-job equipping. This was Jesus' method of producing reproducers, and it's the approach of choice when the stakes are high.

ON-THE-JOB TRAINING

"Ladies and gentlemen, this is your pilot speaking. I'd like to welcome you aboard our flight today. I'm so excited to finally have the chance to fly a real plane! You see, I've been in ground school for several months, and I've learned all about weather, the parts of an airplane, and what all these little gadgets are supposed to do. I thought they would never let me get out here and actually fly, but I'm happy to report that I got an 89 on my final written exam, so they cleared me to start flying! Don't worry; I know exactly what I'm supposed to do. I watched all the instructional videos they showed and didn't miss one day of class."

I don't know about you, but I would quit my last minute pre-flight texting and run out the door as fast as possible! What if the context were an operating room? Imagine lying on the table and hearing your young-looking surgeon exclaim, "Alright! Finally, a living body! I was getting tired of that classroom!" No way am I going to keep lying there! When a job is really important, we don't just train people in the classroom. We equip them for the job through a process that involves both the classroom and practical hands-on experience. Unfortunately, I have seen church after church attempt to train people for just about every aspect of ministry by using only a classroom.

Normally, when church leaders want to train people for small group leadership, what do they do? Hold a class for aspiring small group leaders. What do they do if they want to prepare members for the mission field? Hold a missions class. Training for leadership? Hold a class or conference. We are addicted to the classroom. The church has lost a biblical approach to equipping the body for ministry. What we wouldn't dream of doing when earthly lives are on the line has somehow become standard operating procedure when it comes to dealing with people's eternal souls.

I admit that I have fallen into this trap myself. One of those times was when I was preparing my long-term team to go to Thailand. During our training, we invested time in both the classroom and in practical ministry. The problem arose when I found a book that was particularly helpful in laying out a facilitative approach to ministry. I immediately wanted my whole team to read it and discuss how we might implement the book's principles when we got to the field. If we did what it suggested, our ministry would put a great emphasis on equipping and empowering Thais to do ministry rather than just doing everything ourselves like we had been doing in Birmingham. We all read the book and had great discussions. We spent the next few months finishing raising our support and then our first year in Thailand learning the language. When it came time to actually start doing the ministry, what we did was what we had *done* in Birmingham—doing the ministry ourselves—not what we had *read* in Birmingham—equipping and empowering others to do the ministry. I had violated the equipping principle. People usually remember and repeat what they have done, not what they have heard or read. Books and lectures are helpful, but when it comes to learning skills like flying, surgery, shooting a basketball, or sharing your faith, there is no substitute for hands-on training.

The Master employed this approach when equipping his disciples. Mark reveals Jesus' methodology: "And he appointed twelve (whom he also named apostles) so that they might *be with* him and he might send them out to preach and have authority to cast out demons" (Mark 3:14-15). Why were these twelve invited into Jesus' disciple-making group? To learn how to minister. How would they learn this? By going with Jesus, watching him do it, trying it themselves, and then getting coaching from Jesus on how to improve in the future.

PREREQUSITE TO EQUIPPING

The first step of Jesus' method (be with and watch) raises a really convicting question for me. If someone came to me and asked me to equip him or her for ministry, could I just respond, "Okay, just follow me around and you will learn most of what you need to know"? How about you? Would you dare to give that answer? Before we can embark on the task of equipping others, we must first ask the question, what will people learn from my model? If you wait to start equipping people until you are a perfect example, you will never start. It would be appropriate, though, for us to evaluate our own lives and make the necessary corrections before we challenge people to follow us.

While modeling ministry is of the utmost importance, it is only one step in the equipping process. Expert disciple-makers very deliberately work through all of the steps when training someone. The focus during the equipping stage should be on developing the ministry skills and character needed to lead others. Let's look at those now.

MINISTRY SKILLS DEVELOPMENT

On a beautiful, blue-skied day in July, 1979, I had my first flying lesson. I was a bit surprised when we taxied to the end of the runway and Chopper told me to take the yoke (a plane's steering wheel) because I was going to be performing the takeoff. I hadn't even been to ground school yet, and he was throwing me right into the action! In reality, takeoffs are not all that hard. Landing is a different story, though. When practicing landing, Chopper didn't just talk me through it like he did with the takeoff. No, he landed the plane the first time, letting me watch how he did it. Then we both did it together. Next, I did it as he watched and coached me through it a number of times over the next few weeks. Finally, he told me I was ready to do it by myself. My first solo flight was a bit surreal. When I got up to 1,000 feet, I thought, "What the heck am I doing up here by myself?" My training paid off though, and I put the plane back on the ground in one piece. However, that wasn't the end of my training.

Once on a long cross-country flight, Chopper secretly turned off the fuel valve to see if I would remember my training and respond appropriately when the engine started to sputter and die. In practice, he would reach up and pull the throttle back to idle, saying, "Your engine just failed." I learned in those drills that I need to do the three Fs in the proper order. First, I was to *Fly the Plane*. This meant getting it trimmed out so that it wouldn't lose too much altitude while I did the other Fs. Next, I was to *Find a Field*. Finally, I was to *Fix the Plane*. On that trip, though, when I didn't know he had turned off the fuel, my performance was a mess. When I heard the engine start to die, I looked at Chopper and said, "Oh my goodness, this is for real!" I immediately began to check to see what was wrong with the plane. It wasn't long before I found the fuel valve turned off. I yelled at Chopper, "You sneaky jerk!" He shot back at me, "Don't yell at me, you're the one who just lost 500 feet because you were so busy trying to *Fix the Plane* that you forgot to *Fly the Plane!*" He was right. I had messed up. One thing is for sure, though, I will never forget that lesson. I'm glad his equipping process included follow-up checks and coaching.

The same equipping method Chopper used to teach me the skills of flying can be used to teach someone something as simple as tying one's shoes or as complex as doing brain surgery. The training method is universally applicable wherever a skill needs to be mastered. It should be no surprise that we see Jesus equipping his disciples for ministry in the same way. Let's break it down into a few memorable steps: I Do, We Do, You Do, I Leave, I Check In.

HOW TO EQUIP IN MINISTRY SKILLS

I DO (YOU WATCH)

- *Flying example:* Chopper landed the plane while I watched how he did it.
- *Jesus' example:* The disciples watched Jesus do miracles.
- *Your ministry:* You lead a disciple-making team meeting.

WE DO (TOGETHER)

- *Flying example:* We both had our hands on the yoke and landed the plane together.
- *Jesus' example:* The disciples took part in the feeding of the masses.
- *Your ministry:* You and your disciple co-lead a disciple-making team meeting.

YOU DO (I WATCH)

- *Flying example:* I landed the plane, and Chopper watched and gave feedback.
- *Jesus' example:* The disciples could not cast out a demon, and Jesus had to help and coach them through their failure.
- *Your ministry:* Your disciple leads a disciple-making team meeting, and you give feedback when it is over.

I LEAVE (TRY IT BY YOURSELF)

- *Flying example:* Chopper did not continue flying with me forever. My formal training came to an end, so I got to start taking family and friends for rides.
- *Jesus' example:* After giving the disciples a final charge, he turned things over to them and ascended.
- *Your ministry:* You stop attending their disciple-making team meeting and give them full control.

I CHECK IN (PERIODICALLY CHECK AND SEE IF THEY NEED ANYTHING)

- *Flying example:* Pilots are required to take a "check-ride" every other year to make sure they haven't slipped in their skills.

- *Jesus' example:* Jesus left, but he still corrects through his Spirit and his church, providing resources to his workers when they call on him. (We also see Paul checking back in on disciples to see if correction or resources are needed.)
- *Your ministry:* You check back in with your disciples and see if they need correction, further instruction, or resources.

I have seen some very strong disciple-making ministries grow weaker with each succeeding generation because they failed to practice this crucial final step. Early on in my own ministry, there were a couple of cases where I intentionally did not check in on those I had discipled. Why? I thought that checking back would imply that I didn't trust them or couldn't let go of control. Basically, I thought "ascending" like Jesus meant totally checking out. In reality, we can't send our spirits to encourage and correct like Jesus does. We need to follow Paul's example of going back and visiting those we leave. The feeling I gave those disciples I "ascended" from was not the feeling of trust for which I had hoped. Instead, they felt uncared for and abandoned.

HOW TO CONDUCT A HELPFUL MINISTRY VISIT

Whether you go back and visit the disciple-making ministry of someone you discipled in the past or are just having a coaching meeting with someone you are currently leading, I have found this simple method is helpful. First, I try to meet with as many people in the leader's discipleship chain as possible. This chain or tree may be several generations deep, and meeting with at least someone at each level will prove helpful. The purpose of these meetings is not to coach them, but to ask a lot of questions. Be as encouraging as possible. Then, I meet with the leader one-on-one. During that time, I try to follow an outline using the vowels A.E.I.O.U.

Affirm: Start off the meeting with a hug or a handshake, a smile and a few words affirming some positive things you have seen in the person's life or ministry.

Encourage in the Lord: I usually share something the Lord has been teaching me or encouraging me with lately instead of saying, "This is what I think you need to hear from the Word." It seems less preachy and more powerful that way.

Inspire with the vision: I take the indirect route in this by sharing a story of how I have seen God working lately and possibly in their discipleship tree.

Offer suggestions and help: If you do this in the right spirit, people won't feel you are meddling; they will feel appreciative and empowered.

Uplift in prayer: Before leaving the meeting, I try to ask for prayer requests and spend time praying with them and for them.

Hopefully, understanding the training process we have outlined will help you develop people's ministry skills. While mastering ministry skills is crucial, it's not enough. I know people who possess wonderful skills, and yet I would not want to follow them because of their immaturities. Character development *must* be a major focus during the equipping stage of disciple-making.

CHARACTER DEVELOPMENT

Stop and reflect for a moment. Who are the three people who have most impacted your life for Christ? Now, think about what it was about them that impacted you so deeply. Was it their ministry skills (what you saw them do) or their character (what you saw in them)? I have been asking this question to various groups for almost thirty years, and the response is almost always the same. Nine out of ten people will answer, "character." This corresponds with the scriptural emphasis on character we see in the lists of qualifications for leadership found in 1 Timothy and Titus. Let's look at this breakdown in the following table:

sarah ainsworth love for the Lord
Bompa - character + surrender
Kerry + Jon: commitment to discipleship + life together

Character	Ministry Skill
1 Timothy 3	
Above reproach The husband of one wife Sober-minded Self-controlled Respectable Hospitable Not a drunkard Not violent, but gentle Not quarrelsome Not a lover of money Not a recent convert (not puffed up with conceit) Well thought of by outsiders	Ability to teach (also a character issue) Ability to manage his family and the church (also a character issue)
Additional requirements found in Titus 1	
A lover of good Upright Holy Holds firmly to the Word	

Helping people grow in godly character must be a major focus of the equipping phase of disciple-making. If it is true that "more is caught than taught," then who we are in our character is of the utmost importance. Whether we like it or not, we reproduce after our own kind. It is unrealistic to think that the men I am discipling will have the heart and actions of a servant if I, their leader, don't display those in my own life. More than that, how would I ever reprove them for a lack of servanthood if I know I have not modeled it for them? Equipping people for ministry means helping them grow in Christ-likeness. Unfortunately, most of the emphasis in leadership development focuses on helping people *know* more. It almost completely ignores character development. Right action and right character do not flow from wrong beliefs. Teaching solid doctrine is essential, but if an emphasis on the passing along of knowledge through lecture-style teaching would bring about godly disciple-makers, then our churches would be full of them.

I am convinced that God's individualized sanctification plan for each one of us extends way beyond the work of any one mentor in our lives.[48] His plan includes things that grow us in character, such as suffering and his discipline. However, he wants each of us to engage in the process of helping others reach a higher level of Christ-likeness. Notice in the following verse that Paul and his fellow workers don't merely proclaim Christ, they strive to bring each person to maturity in Christ: "Him we proclaim, warning everyone and teaching everyone with all wisdom, that we may present everyone mature in Christ. For this I toil, struggling with all his energy that he powerfully works within me" (Colossians 1:28-29). How exactly do we do this?

HELPING OTHERS GROW IN CHARACTER

Although God is sovereign in the salvation and sanctification of his people, he graciously allows us to join him in this transforming process. When we engage in *Evangelizing* and see the Lord bring someone to himself, we have taken the first step toward witnessing someone grow in Christ-like character.[49] During the *Establishing* stage, we help young disciples become more like Christ by teaching them to self-feed on God's Word and to obey all that he commands them by walking in the power of the Holy Spirit. While obedience to his commands is a must, I believe that nothing is more transformative than seeing the face of God in Christ.[50] Over and over again in Scripture, the writers use the character of God as the motivating factor for character change.

> Be merciful, *even as your Father* is merciful. (Luke 6:36)

> Therefore welcome one another *as Christ has* welcomed you, for the glory of God. (Romans 15:7)

> ...forgiving each other; *as the Lord* has forgiven you, so you also must forgive. (Colossians 3:13b)

> ...since it is written, "You shall be holy, *for I am holy*." (1 Peter 1:16)

There is no more powerful force in existence for character change than to see the beauty of him who is holy in all his attributes. We cannot see God and remain unchanged. As author A.W. Tozer writes, "We tend by a secret law of the soul to move toward [to be formed after] our mental image of God."[51] Many times I find myself frustrated with the inaction and apparent lack of concern many churchgoers have for the billions of people who have never heard the gospel. It is tempting to diagnose their problem as worldliness, lack of compassion, selfishness, or fear. The truth is, however, that our greatest need is to know God better, for when we are saturated with the knowledge of him, ungodliness and inaction are not an option. As the prophet Daniel says, "…but the people who know their God shall stand firm and take action" (Daniel 11:32).

To help people grow in their knowledge of God and character during the *Establishing* stage, our efforts should focus mostly on getting into place disciplines and environments that will help them recognize areas where they need to grow while giving them the tools to do so. For review, these are:

- Self-feeding on God's Word and hearing the Word preached regularly
- A commitment to obedience
- Learning to walk in the power of the Holy Spirit
- Living in Christian community
- Hungering for and pursuing the knowledge of God
- Walking in the freedom Christ provides
- Personal evaluation and getting close friends' input on strengths and weaknesses

Think about the people you are discipling in light of the above list. Do you see any deficiencies that you could help them with? If you help them with these now, you will be putting them into a growth posture for the future. When these things are in place, tremendous character progress occurs without any special intervention from you. Remember the old adage: "Give a man a fish and he will eat for a day. Teach a man to fish and he will eat for a lifetime." That's what you will be doing in respect to their character development. The Holy Spirit will use these components to bring about conviction of sin and the repentance needed for life change.

At times however, God in his sovereignty chooses to leave certain areas of our immaturity as blind spots or stubborn strongholds that require the intervention of other believers. When Christ performed the miracle of calling Lazarus from death to life, he did not cause all of his old smelly grave clothes to fall off of him. He commanded others to help him get free from his "junk," if you will. "The man who had died came out, his hands and feet bound with linen strips, and his face wrapped with a cloth. Jesus said to them, 'Unbind him, and let him go'" (John 11:44). This illustrates well what Jesus taught elsewhere. For example, Jesus commanded us to help each other get rid of sin in our lives when he commanded us to wash each other's feet (John 13). Jesus is using the washing of dirt from one another's feet as a metaphor for helping each other in the sanctification process. We don't help each other with our positional holiness; Christ has already taken care of that and made us "completely clean" (John 13:10). However, we do help each other clean up the sins of our daily walks. Sometimes this requires pointing out to one another specific sins and character immaturities that have not been noticed or successfully addressed in the *Establishing* stage.[52] As you can see, training disciples becomes more individualized in the *Equipping* stage and will require more one-on-one time. If you have selected at this point only those who have shown themselves faithful to pass along what they have learned, you can be assured that this will be time well spent. Let's look now at how to help others grow in specific areas of character.

HOW TO HELP OTHERS DEAL WITH A SPECIFIC CHARACTER IMMATURITY

When I was a college sophomore, someone other than my parents tried to lovingly help me grow in a specific area of character. My discipleship leader, Jay, asked me if I could stop by his dorm room because he wanted to talk. When I arrived, he pulled out a 3x5 card on which he had jotted a few notes. Jay proceeded to say, "Bob, you know I love you, and because I do, I want to talk with you about something. I think you have a problem with pride. You know that the Bible says that 'God opposes the proud but gives grace to the humble.'" Then he went on to share with me a few examples of how he had seen pride manifest itself in my speech and actions. Ouch! Even though it was hard to listen to and a bit embarrassing, I didn't push back on it because his examples were pretty clear, and I knew his motives were pure. Jay then assured me that he would help me grow in this area and that he was committed to our friendship.

Step One: Take the log out of your own eye.

The place to start helping someone else grow in an area of character is to make sure you are modeling growth in that area yourself. Remember that modeling is your most powerful teaching tool. You don't have to be perfect in an area before you can confront someone else about it, but you must at least be progressing. If you're not, it would be hypocritical to tell them they need to grow in that area.

Step Two: Help them see it.

Everyone has blind spots, and just identifying them can do tremendous good. I remember when I was sixteen and learning to fly. My flight instructor, nicknamed "Chopper," confronted me about being overly confident. He said, "Bob, there are old pilots and bold pilots, but no old bold pilots." He then pointed out how I rushed my pre-flight examination of the plane. I respected Chopper, and his examples were true. Simply pointing out my weaknesses made a big impression on me. It caused me to change my attitude and habits. Here is a method I use when I need to confront people.

- Pray it through first.
- Go to them privately.
- Affirm your love for them.
- State the problem in a sentence (I suggest writing it out on a 3x5 card).
- Share a verse (at the most two) on the subject to show God's standard.

- Give a few specific examples but not so many as to crush. (If you can only think of one, than maybe it is not a trend in their life and you don't need to point it out. We all have bad moments that aren't characteristic of us, right?)
- Offer to help them grow in this area in any way they would like.
- Assure them of your ongoing commitment to them.

Step Three: Encourage them to get into the Word about it.

The Bible has a lot to say about character issues. Think about all the verses on pride, fear, greed, complaining, selfishness, laziness, etc. We are transformed by the renewing of our minds.[53] Renewal starts with time in God's Word.

Step Four: Help them apply what they learn in the Word.

Bible knowledge is not enough. Life change comes from applying what we learn. But sometimes people don't make their application steps nearly specific enough to act on. Here is a conversation that illustrates how you can help someone think through the application of God's Word:

> **Leader:** What did you learn from your study on selfishness this week?
>
> **Disciple:** I kept seeing over and over again that true love is willing to sacrifice for others.
>
> **Leader:** Great! Have you thought about how to apply that in your daily life?
>
> **Disciple:** Yes, I am going to try to be less selfish and serve others more.
>
> **Leader:** That's good, but it is a little bit general. Can you think of some specific situations where you tend to be selfish and what you can do serve at those times?
>
> **Disciple:** Well, I know I sit and watch T.V. when my wife is doing household chores. I guess I could get up and help her.
>
> **Leader:** That's a great idea. Would you like me to ask you next week how it went?

This conversation demonstrates how to lovingly take a biblical principle and funnel it into a specific action step of obedience. Remember, our job is to help people walk in obedience to what they read in the Bible, and specific steps are crucial to seeing this happen.

Step Five: Give them appropriate homework assignments.

A friend of mine was extremely shy as a college student. You would never know that about him now because a mentor in his life recognized this and gave him a challenge to greet ten new people in a week. I love to hear him tell the story of how he struggled to do it. The week was almost over. It was 9:00

PM. on Sunday night, and he still had to greet eight more people, so he got in his car and drove down to the grocery store. Halfway down aisle one, he saw someone and mustered up the courage to look at him and say "Hi." Then, he went to aisle two and found a lady to greet. He found someone else on aisle four, but the rest of the store was empty because it was late. So he decided to buy something so he could greet the cashier. Still being short of his goal, he visited a gas station to buy some gum. I think before the night was over he had visited every gas station in the area and had enough gum to last him for a year, but he was growing because a mentor took a risk, brought up the issue, and gave him an appropriate assignment. Can you think of an assignment you might suggest to one of the people you are discipling? If someone who knows you well were to think of an assignment that would help you, what do you think it would be? How about asking some trusted friends to hold you to it? Wouldn't that be a great example for those you are discipling and set the stage for you to suggest an assignment for them?

Step Six: Be there to help them if they fail to make progress.

When people fail to make much progress, I will usually do one or all of the following:

- Offer to guide them through a half day of prayer that focuses on repentance and engaging in spiritual warfare.[54]
- Provide ongoing encouragement.
- Suggest that they visit a professional Christian counselor if progress continues to be elusive.

How we train people and the areas we focus on with them are important, but *whom* we select to equip can be even more determinative of whether multiplication takes place or not. The best training in the world, done with the wrong people, will not produce reproducers.

WHOM TO EQUIP

Poor selection of disciples to equip is the most common mistake I have seen in spiritual reproduction, and it is a fatal one. Fortunately, looking closely at how Jesus went about selection and properly understanding Paul's instructions to Timothy on the subject will help us avoid the deadly trap of selecting people who are not ready for equipping.

JESUS' PROCEDURE FOR SELECTION

I taught a seminary class for a number of years on the subject of discipleship. When we came to the topic of selection, I gave my students what has proven to be a particularly enlightening homework assignment. Using a harmony of the gospels, they had to make a list of all that Jesus did from the time he started his ministry until the moment he selected the twelve apostles.[55] I think many of them were astounded by what they discovered. Jesus didn't select the twelve for leadership equipping until he had done a lot of broad ministry and had a chance to see which of his disciples really meant business.[56] Below is a list of ministry activities Jesus engaged in before he ever selected the twelve men he would equip.

- Jesus spent forty days and nights in prayer and fasting before starting his ministry. (Matthew 4:1-11)
- Jesus spent time with potential disciples (Andrew and Peter). (John 1:35-51)
- Jesus spoke with more potential disciples (Philip and Nathanael). (John 1:43-51)
- Jesus went to a social event (wedding) with his disciples. He did a miracle (turned water into wine) and then spent a few days with disciples and family together. (John 2:1-12)
- Jesus drove merchants out of the temple. (John 2:13-19)
- Jesus did miraculous signs in view of many people. (John 2:23)
- Jesus evangelized Nicodemus. (John 3:1-21)
- Jesus spent time with his disciples in the Judean countryside and baptized people. (John 3:22-24)
- Jesus gained more disciples, and he let his disciples baptize (get involved in the ministry). He traveled to minister in different places with his disciples. (John 4:1-3)
- Jesus witnessed to the woman at the well. (John 4:4-26)
- Jesus taught his disciples about spiritual food, cast a vision for the harvest, and stayed in the village to teach the Samaritans. (John 4:27-42)

- Jesus healed the official's son from a distance. (John 4: 46-54)
- Jesus performed a miracle (large catch of fish). (Luke 5:1-9)
- Jesus invited them to train to become fishers of men. Several disciples left their nets and followed him. (Matt. 4:19)
- Jesus taught at the synagogue and cast out demons. (Mark 1:21-28)
- Jesus went to disciples' homes. (Mark 1:29-31)
- Jesus healed more people and cast out more demons. (Mark 1:32-34)
- The disciples saw Jesus have a quiet time. (Mark 1:35)
- Jesus went with the disciples to other villages to preach. (Mark 1:38-39)
- Jesus cleansed a leper and healed a paralytic. (Mark 1:40-2:12)
- Jesus preached the good news of the kingdom and healed more people. Crowds followed him. (Matt. 4:23-25)
- Jesus taught large crowds by the lake. He challenged Levi to follow him and then ate dinner at Levi's house with many "sinners." (Mark 2:13-17)
- Jesus taught further, and he and his disciples witnessed opposition. He defended the disciples eating grain and healed the hand of a man in the synagogue. (Mark 2:18-3:6)
- Jesus healed a man at the Pool of Bethesda. (John 5:1-9)
- Jesus withdrew with his disciples and then healed many. (Mark 3:7-10)
- Jesus spent the night in prayer. (Luke 6:12)
- Jesus called twelve to "be with him" to "send them out to preach." (Mark 3:14)

From the very beginning of his ministry, Jesus called many people to follow him as his disciples and to participate in the mission of God as "fishers of men."[57] Notice that he didn't say to people, "Come, follow me, and I will help you grow." He didn't have to because growth would be automatic. As Pastor David Platt often says, "God's got this thing rigged. When we start evangelizing and discipling others, we end up growing more than they do."

Jesus sowed the seed of the gospel broadly, teaching many in large groups that we might today call his "Bible studies." This should not be confused with his specific selection of the twelve whom he poured his life into for leadership equipping. He did not make this selection until he was into the middle of his second year of ministry.[58] We know that one of the qualifications for Apostleship was that one had to have been with Jesus since the time of the baptism of John, which was at the beginning of Jesus' ministry.[59] So, if the men Jesus eventually selected to "be with him" and receive his focused ministry equipping had been around since the beginning of his ministry, why did Jesus wait more than a year to challenge them into this special relationship?[60] It could be that these men weren't ready yet for this type of intense relationship. Perhaps Jesus wanted time to observe those who were following him to see which individuals were being faithful to pass on what they were being taught. Maybe it was because Jesus wanted to model for us how to go about the selection process. There is wisdom in following the Master's disciple-making pattern of ministering to and with many before selecting the few on whom we will focus our disciple-making efforts. If Jesus, who is God, went about selection this way, it would be safe for us to say that *selection without observation is presumption.*

Aspiring disciple-makers often go too narrowly too soon, and, as a result, don't find the key people through whom they could really multiply their lives. Jesus' model for starting a ministry was not *"start small, think big, go deep."* It was *"start big, think small, go deep."* If you want to disciple three or four people, don't start with three or four people. Start a disciple-making team with twelve! The most effective disciple-makers we studied discipled an average of four people yet led larger cell groups of eight to twelve people.

It is important to keep in mind that, within the group of twelve, Jesus selected three key men (Peter, James and John) for even more intense leadership development. Some of the most highly effective churches in existence today use this same principle in selecting people for leadership equipping. In these churches, small group leaders are challenged to carefully observe those in their cell (a small group of eight to fifteen people), watching for signs of faithfulness in passing along what they are receiving. They then select between one to three apprentices out of their cell groups whom they will equip to launch disciple-making teams of their own. Maintaining the larger cell group allows the leader to have a pool of people from which to observe and choose future leaders. The wise leader also asks the apprentices to help with ministry to the rest of the group. This provides an ideal environment for modeling, delegating, coaching, and feedback.

PAUL'S INSTRUCTIONS ON SELECTION

The apostle Paul's disciple-making instructions to Timothy contain vital principles for avoiding spiritual sterility: "and what you have heard from me in the presence of many witnesses entrust to faithful men who will be able to teach others also" (2 Timothy 2:2). There are two qualifications Paul mentions to look for in people you will choose to equip: faithfulness and the ability to teach others.

FAITHFULNESS

When I first started discipling men, I misunderstood the area of faithfulness I was to look for. I thought identifying faithfulness meant finding someone who would show up to our meetings on time with his homework completed. Those would be important things to look for if you are searching for a good student, but the objective mentioned in 2 Timothy 2:2 was reproduction. Paul wanted Timothy to pick some men who wouldn't be dead ends. They should instead keep the process going—men who would be faithful to take what they had learned and pass it on to others. Think of a relay race. Paul had passed the baton to Timothy, and he wanted Timothy to pick men who would be "faithful" to pass it on to others, not men who would be distracted by "civilian affairs" or become disqualified by unrighteous behavior (v. 3-5).

Over the years I've noticed that often the men who are most faithful in sharing what they have learned aren't always the ones who show up to meetings on time with all their homework completed. Their passion for people and ministry sometimes causes time-management problems. Regardless, I would rather spend my time investing in a "mover and shaker" than in a man who shows up on time with his homework completed yet never does anything with it.

When I first started discipling people, I would find someone I thought would be a good candidate, and then I would sit him down and challenge him to a discipling relationship with me. During the conversation, I would challenge him to be F.A.T.—Faithful, Available, and Teachable. This was a horrible idea. You want F.A.T. disciples, but when it comes to selecting people to equip, your job is not to challenge people to be something they aren't. Instead, I should have picked men who already met the qualifications. To do this, you will need plenty of time to observe them. This is the model that Jesus gave us. So minister broadly and don't hurry the selection process. If you will lead a small group of eight to fifteen people and continually engage in team evangelism with those in the group, it will become clear to you which people would be the best to challenge into a deeper discipling relationship. You should equip everyone in the group in evangelism without imposing selection criteria. Next, see who is faithful to use what they have been given. Those who have been faithful with the little you have given them should be given more of your time and further equipping. In a sense, you are not really selecting them. They are selecting themselves.

ABILITY TO TEACH OTHERS

The men Timothy chose didn't just need the desire and resolve to teach others; they had to have the ability to do so. Certainly, this ability must include the capability to teach God's Word to at least a few other people. In a discipling ministry, however, the need isn't so much public speaking ability as it is a record of personal credibility. No one is perfect, but without what author Allen Hadidian calls "a life worth emulating," no one will want to listen to what you have to say.[61] That is why Paul points out, "An athlete is not crowned unless he competes according to the rules" (2 Timothy 2:5). Unfortunately, we have all seen a lack of personal holiness disqualify people from the disciple-making race. Thankfully, with true repentance and growth, it is a contest that can be re-entered by the grace of God.

PRACTICAL APPLICATION

So how do we put these principles of selection into practice today? Don't try to start your discipling ministry by going out and asking three or four people into your group. Instead, challenge about twelve people with the vision of being a disciple-making team; a team that would begin by evangelizing together as a team with the end goal of multiplying disciples. Both the *Missional Community Study Guide* that goes with this book and the *Foundations Missional Community Guidebook* are designed to help you do that.[62] By starting your ministry this way, you would be doing something similar to what Jesus did when he began his ministry by challenging men with the call to "Come, follow me, and I will make you fishers of men" (Matthew 4:19). Then, after you have been together for a while and can see who is faithful, ask a few in your group into a special equipping relationship. The focus of your time with your few apprentices will be on helping them to develop their character and ministry skills. Do you see how this suggestion is vastly different than the "Hey, would you like to start meeting at a coffee shop and I will disciple you" model? Hopefully the following table will help you see those differences. Here is a comparison between the two approaches:

Coffee Shop Model	Jesus' Model
Start by ministering to a few	Start by ministering to many
Call men to join you in a meeting	Call men to join you in evangelism
Goal: make disciples	Goal: make disciple-makers
Focus: growth	Focus: multiplication
Assumption: personal growth will lead to ministry	Assumption: ministry will lead to personal growth
Selection occurs at the beginning of ministry	Selection occurs after seeing who is faithful
Discipling takes place apart from evangelism	Discipling takes place in the context of evangelism
Curriculum: emphasizes knowledge	Curriculum: emphasizes character and skills

DURATION OF DISCIPLING

Once we have selected faithful people and challenged them to join us in mission, how long should we disciple them? Is longer better? Do you ever graduate from the need for discipling? Should you always have a disciple in your life?

Jesus was with his disciples for three years, and about half of that time was after he chose the twelve apostles. Is that the right amount of time for us with our modern lifestyles? Is quality more important than duration in the discipling relationship? We wondered those same things so we asked our survey participants two questions:

1. How many months were you formally discipled?
2. How would you evaluate your experience of being discipled?

From their answers we discovered the following:

- It is important to be formally discipled for at least some length of time. Of those who had never been discipled, over 80 percent were non-effective.
- There was a higher than expected occurrence of effectiveness among people who were discipled for about three years. Looks like Jesus knew what he was doing when he allowed his disciples to follow him for about three years!
- There is very strong support for a connection between the *quality* of the discipling relationship and effectiveness in reproducing.

REMINDER

Even well-equipped people will struggle to be fruitful and may even discontinue ministry if they are not part of a disciple-making team. Receiving equipping in evangelism is important, but there is no evidence that effectiveness increases proportionally with the amount of training received. Being in an evangelism training program is very helpful because it provides things like ongoing vision, modeling, coaching, teamwork, prayer, and structure. Disciple-makers who said they were a part of a small group that spent at least twenty minutes weekly discussing evangelism, twenty minutes praying for the lost, and twenty minutes doing some sort of evangelism together are far more effective than those who didn't. Putting all of this together further clarifies that one of the most important things we can do to equip our disciples to reproduce is not necessarily to train them further. Instead, we need to make sure they understand how to function together with others as a disciple-making team and develop a deep commitment to do so for the rest of their lives.

Equipping someone to labor in the harvest is not the end of the disciple-making process. What good would it do to train a bunch of harvesters and then never get them into the ripe fields that are in need of workers? We must finish the work we began and join with Jesus in *Exporting* disciple-makers into areas where they are needed most. I'll share with you in the next chapter what got me started on the most amazing journey of my life.

THE MULTIPLICATION CYCLE

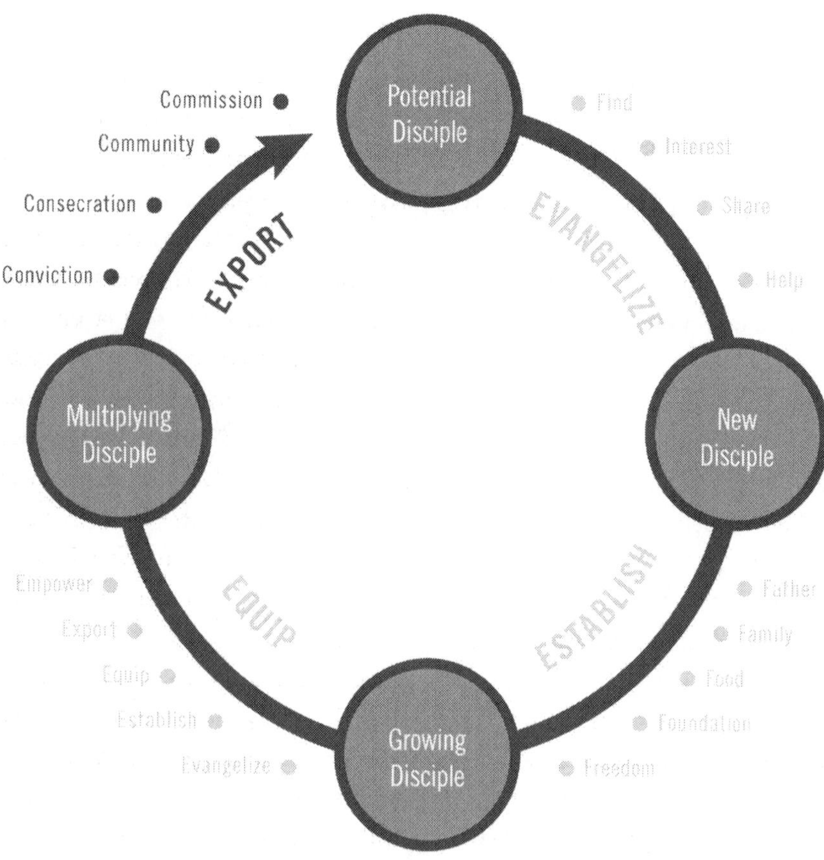

CHAPTER 9

THE LOST ASPECT OF DISCIPLE-MAKING

[EXPORTING]

When I was a college student, I opened a small pamphlet not knowing what to expect. I was planning to scan it quickly then throw it away. Instead, I ended up giving my life to its message. The pamphlet was titled *Why You Should Go to the Mission Field.*[63] Most stunning to me were the statistics it shared. It reported that our world had over 2.7 billion people who had never heard the gospel even once, and that 80,000 lost people were dying and going to hell every day. It pointed out that the number of Avon and Amway representatives in America was fourteen times the number of missionaries representing Jesus worldwide. Most disturbing of all, it said that in America we had one Christian worker for every 230 people. In the rest of the world, that number was one worker for every 450,000. These statistics made me wonder, "How could this be? What happened? How could there be such an imbalance in the distribution of laborers in the world? Has the church lost the aspect of disciple-making called '*Exporting*' (mobilizing, deploying, sending)?"

If the statistics I was reading were true, I could not just sit and do nothing. I had to talk with someone, but whom? The only missionary I had ever met was my Old Testament professor, so I asked him to go to lunch and tell me more about missions. He shared with me an old missionary story that illustrated the problem of an imbalanced mission force and the need for a response on my part. The illustration went like this: Imagine you are going to a sawmill to work. When you arrive, you see ten men lifting one end of a giant log and one man by himself on the other end. To which end of the log would you go? I said, "I would go to the end where I am most needed, of course." Immediately the implications for missions were clear. I began to reason, "In light of the great imbalance of laborers in the world and the command to go to *all* nations, I should head where the laborers are few unless God gives me some kind of special communication telling me *not* to go. I should assume I am to go unless he tells me otherwise." When it comes to the idea of needing a special missionary call, Jim Elliot put it this way: "Why do you need a voice when you have a verse?" Up to this point I had been willing to go, but planning to stay. In light of this new information, I committed to flip that. I needed to plan to go and be willing to stay.

SEEING THE NEED FIRSTHAND

While this information had impacted my mind and brought a change in my plans, it did not become a vivid, heart-checking reality until I saw firsthand the consequences of disciple-makers failing to export. This happened while I was a campus minister at a small college in Alabama. I had taken the job because I committed not to go to the unreached alone. I wanted to mobilize others to go with me and multiply my impact. I used to walk the streets and sidewalks of the campus at night and cry out to God, asking him to raise up men and women who would join me as a team to go to those who had never heard. Exactly where, though, I didn't know. I had spent a summer in Korea and knew that I didn't want to go back. The Korean people were wonderful, but I saw there were plenty of churches there already. My ambition was not just to go overseas, but to go to the end of the log where I was truly needed.

I finally received my chance to get among the unreached after my second year of full-time ministry when my boss asked me to spend a few weeks in Thailand with some of the students from my ministry. After a twenty-eight hour trip from Alabama and a few days in Bangkok, our team took a twelve-hour sleeper train to the north of Thailand. From there, we loaded onto buses and headed east for about four hours, finally loading into the backs of six four-wheel drive pick-up trucks that carried us up muddy mountain roads for another two hours. When we finally arrived at the remote jungle village, two thoughts ran through my mind. The first was that any minute John Rambo should be popping out from behind one of the bamboo houses with a big knife and some emaciated POWs. The second thought was that I had finally arrived at the place I had heard about in Sunday school for so many years—"the uttermost parts of the world." The next forty-eight hours clarified for me on a heart level what our failure to export disciples really means and the injustice that it brings.

The village had 280 people living in it. Their primitive houses surrounded a soccer field and small school building. With the permission of the village headman, we hung a sheet from one of the soccer goals and set up our projector and generator to show the *Jesus* film. Do you have any idea how many of these animists showed up to see a film about Jesus? Two hundred and eighty! That is 100 percent of the village population. If we showed up with a film in your neighborhood, what percentage of your neighbors do you think would show up? Most likely, not many. Why? Many of your neigbors have heard about Jesus before. That's the point! We need to take the good news to those who have never heard it before.

After such an amazing turnout the first night, we decided to show it again the next night. Can you guess how many people showed up? Two hundred and eighty! "Wait a minute, Bob, maybe they were just bored and not really coming because they were interested in Jesus." I can see how you might think that if you didn't know about some of the reactions we received after the movie. For example, on the ride up to the village, a missionary named Chip shared the gospel with one of the truck drivers and gave him a *Four Spiritual Laws* booklet in Thai. After the movie the first night, the truck driver came up to Chip with the other five drivers and told him, "They just watched the movie and want you to tell them what you told me. And they want to know if you have any more of those booklets." The day after we showed the movie the first time, we were doing some manual labor in the village. One of the village ladies was working alongside us, and during a break, she worked up the courage to ask Chip, "If someone wanted to know Jesus, what would he or she have to do?" After Chip explained the gospel to her, she commented, "You know, I think a lot of people in my village would want to know Jesus, but we just don't know enough. If someone could stay here and teach us more..." That came like a dagger to my heart because I knew we were leaving the next day. Later, as we were busy working, a half-dressed man who lived in a shelter made of banana leaves in the jungle wandered into the village. He explained that for two weeks he had been praying that if God were real, he would send someone to explain how to know him. He wanted to know if we had come to tell people about God.

About halfway through the film on the second night, I got up from my grassy seat and headed back to check the gas in the generator that powered the projector. As I walked through these people who were sitting and watching the movie for the second time, the events of the past two days came crashing down. The *Jesus* film was on the screen behind me, but in my mind, I could see two screens flashing different images. On one of the screens were the events of the past forty-eight hours: 100 percent of the village showing up two nights in a row to hear about Jesus. Six truck drivers asking for gospel tracts. The banana leaf guy from the jungle searching for God. The lady saying that a lot of people in her village would want to know Jesus if we could just stay and teach them more. On the other screen ran thoughts of a fraternity house and students back home who had told me that they didn't want to hear me share about Jesus because they had already heard about him so many times. I thought about churches where I had preached back in the States in which the people had become inoculated against the gospel because of their repeated exposure and lack of response to it. Then, somewhere before reaching the generator, I just began to weep. I thought, "This is so unfair. Why do some people get so many opportunities to hear the gospel, while others never get a single chance to say yes to Jesus?"

Was it God's fault, or had *we* failed so miserably to export those we had raised up? If it was our fault, why had we failed to mobilize laborers when the command and need are so clear?

THE FAILURE CONTINUES

More than twenty-five years later, the failure to export disciple-makers continues. There are certain areas of the world today that have laborers stacked and packed while others have virtually none. For example, my home state of Alabama has a population of 4.7 million. Sixty-seven percent meet the criteria to be considered "born again."[64] If just 10 percent of those believers actually labor for Christ, the number of workers in Alabama would still be an astounding 315,000! That's one laborer for every five Alabamians who are not born again. Part of me says, "Praise God for what he has done in Alabama!" But another part of me says, "Something doesn't seem right, considering there are only a handful of laborers trying to reach more than 128 million Shaikh people in Bangladesh."[65]

How could this have happened? As an old Navigator staff member once told me, "Laborers are like manure. It stinks when they are all piled up in one place. You have to spread them out to do any good." We all agree with this. No one would argue with the idea that laborers need to be spread out. However, some may question the claim that *you* have to spread them out. After all, isn't making disciples our part and sending them out God's part? If this distinction is true, then the great imbalance is a result of God failing to do his part. Obviously, this can't be true, so we need to reexamine our practices. Could it be that while we have worked hard to *Evangelize* the lost, *Establish* them in their faith, and *Equip* them to labor, we have ended the intentional discipling process too soon? Have we failed to finish the job by not *Exporting* more of those we have equipped? We indeed have an active role to play in *Exporting*.

THE BIBLICAL BASIS FOR EXPORTING

Jesus commands us in Matthew 28:19 to "make disciples" and in Matthew 9:38 to "pray earnestly to the Lord of the harvest to send out laborers." A quick reading of these two commands, without considering the rest of Scripture, could lead to the conclusion that our job is to "make disciples," and God's job is to send them out. Is this true?

Jesus didn't say anything about praying in Matthew 28 when he commanded us to make disciples. Does that mean that we can make disciples without prayer? Of course not. I can't think of any activity in the Christian life that we should attempt without prayer. Activity without prayer usually doesn't end well. What about prayer without activity? That doesn't result in much fruit either.

Paul says in 1 Corinthians that we need both human activity and dependence on God to see fruit: "I planted the seed, Apollos watered it, but God made it grow" (1 Corinthians 3:6). If God doesn't want us to *Evangelize, Establish,* or *Equip* disciples by prayer alone, why would we think he wants us to become passive in the *Exporting* process and do nothing but pray?

After Jesus emphasized to his disciples the need for prayer in regard to the mobilization of laborers (Matthew 9:38), what did he do? He sent them out. We must admit that the great imbalance of laborers in the world is not a result of God failing to do his part, but a result of us failing to do ours. We need to heed the admonition I was given on a placard years ago, *"Be like Jesus. Love the world's lost people enough to send them disciple-makers."* Perhaps part of the reason we haven't done this more is that we just haven't understood some of the keys to successfully mobilizing laborers. The rest of this chapter lays out four keys to exporting that will help you walk with your disciples through the process of becoming World Christians.

KEYS TO GROWING AND EXPORTING WORLD CHRISTIANS

KEY ONE: CONVICTION

We must help those we are leading to develop a conviction from God's Word that they need to align their lives with God's global purposes. How should we go about that, though?

One would think that, with more than two million teens going on short-term trips annually, mission agencies would be flooded with interested people.[66] In reality, though, short-term trips are not leading to long-term goers. Over the past few years I have asked several mission agencies what leads to long-term workers. One responded that it was not short-term trips that new workers cited as the reason they sought long-term service. He said that over 90 percent decided to pursue long-term missions after taking the *Perspectives on the World Christian Movement* course.[67] When I shared this comment with other mission agencies, they agreed and responded that they are seeing the same thing with their applicants. What is so powerful about this course? The first five weeks are devoted to laying down *The Biblical Perspective* on mission from Genesis to Revelation. Conviction from God's Word is a powerful tool in exporting laborers to the lost world.

These conversations confirm what mission mobilizer Bob Sjogren says about how he has seen people become interested in going long-term to Muslims. Bob said that when he traveled around preaching only one missions sermon in a location and then moving on, he never saw a lot of interest from people in going. However, when he started teaching a seminar that walked people through the Scriptures from Genesis to Revelation, showing them the grand narrative of the Bible, the number of people wanting to talk with him about going jumped significantly.[68]

One of the most common remarks I hear from people who have finished a *Perspectives* course is, "I will never read my Bible the same way again."

What they mean is that they have seen the grand narrative of Scripture. What used to seem like separate stories now all fit into one larger story of God bringing all nations to himself in Christ. They have begun to read their Bible through a Christ *and* mission-centered lens. When this happens, a deep conviction based on God's unshakable Word will form, and their lives will begin to conform to his will.

UNDERSTANDING THE MANDATE

The mandate is to make disciples of all the ethne (nations). This word *ethne* is the plural form of the Greek word *ethnos*. We get the word *ethnic* from this word. The command is not to merely make disciples in each of the 193 member nations of the United Nations. The command is to make disciples of each of the 16,000 or more distinct people groups of the world. For example, when we think about India as the Great Commission tells us to, we don't see one country, but 2,605 distinct people groups. Because these groups have different heritages, customs, cultures, languages, and geographical locations, the gospel will not necessarily flow easily from one group to the next. There are currently 2,280 of those groups that still need representatives of Christ to cross over into them and proclaim the gospel. Worldwide, the estimate is that there are more than 7,000 people groups (*ethne*) who are still unreached.[69] When Christians see from God's Word that Christ has "...ransomed people for God from every tribe and language and people and nation..." (Revelation 5:9) and does not intend to return until the gospel has been preached in each of them (Matthew 24:14), then they are on their way to gaining a transforming vision for their lives. This insight that the Great Commission is not just about winning a lot of people to Christ, but discipling people from all different nations and people groups, demands that we bring our little stories into alignment with God's big story. While insight is a starting point, it will require consecration on your part and that of your disciples for real world impact to occur.

KEY TWO: CONSECRATION

CULTIVATE AND MODEL A WORLD CHRISTIAN HEART AND LIFESTYLE YOURSELF FIRST

The axiom, "You reproduce after your own kind," holds true here. Worldly Christians do not raise up crops of World Christians. It is preposterous to believe that half-committed leaders will raise up fully-committed followers. What exactly do I mean by "World Christian"? A World Christian is a follower of Jesus who, fueled by his own passionate worship of his Savior, has made God's global purpose of bringing every nation to himself the overmastering and unifying ambition of his life.[70] In fact, he sees it as more important than life itself.[71] Having seen the world through God's eyes, being worldly is not an option. He can no longer live the comfortable, self-absorbed life while billions face an eternity in hell, having never even heard the gospel once. Compartmentalizing missions into a yearly ten-day trip is no longer an option. He has laid his "yes" on the table and told God to put it on the map. He will go wherever, whenever, and work with whomever God tells him. If he does not personally go to the unreached, his commitment to them will be no less. He will live each day to see to it that they come to know the glory of God in Christ.[72] He will pray, mobilize, welcome internationals into his home, and give with all the strength God puts in him. He is vigilant to keep his heart from hardening and losing a passion for Christ and compassion for the lost. Lukewarm mediocrity is not an option. He engages in regular, honest evaluation of his practice of the World Christian lifestyle and sets fresh growth goals repeatedly.

What about you? Would you be willing to evaluate your World Christian development and set goals for your progress? If so, you can use the following evaluation to guide you.

GIVE YOUR DISCIPLES OVER TO THE LORD FOR HIM TO SEND OUT

As a full-time mobilizer, I have had hundreds of conversations with aspiring missionaries who are later derailed in their journey to the unreached. Why? They have been convinced that they are needed too much in their current ministry or that they need more training before they go (some do need more training, but many don't).

Thankfully, I have seen a number of churches and ministries where they don't resist but rather encourage their best laborers to leave for less reached fields. And they don't just preach that from up front and then privately hold back their "A" players and let their "B" and "C" players go. They mobilize their best. Ironically, their ministries grow faster than ministries that recruit their best disciple-makers to stay. God's economy just works that way. The more you lose, the more you gain! What about you? Are you making the gutsy move of sending out your best people?

WORLD CHRISTIAN EVALUATION

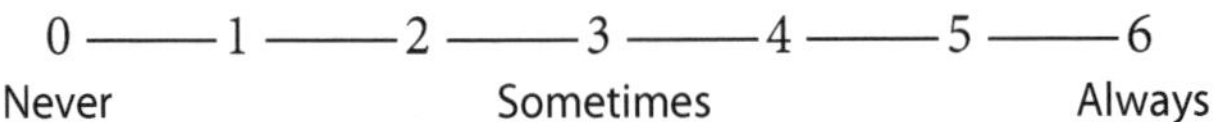

____ I pray for the nations frequently and fervently.
____ I see God's heart for the nations each time I read my Bible.
____ I regularly cast vision for the nations with those I lead.
____ Other people would say that I am passionate for the nations.
____ I eagerly study and read things that will help me better understand and meet the needs of the nations.
____ I intentionally befriend and evangelize internationals.
____ I give sacrificially to world missions.
____ I am personally committed to do all that I can to see to it that the gospel gets not only to the lost, but especially to the unreached.
____ I regularly lay my life before the Lord and volunteer to move anywhere he wants me to go.
____ Current Total *0–18 = Low*
19–32 = Average
33–54 = High
____ Total I would like to grow to in the next twelve months

CHALLENGE THOSE YOU LEAD TO GO WHEREVER GOD LEADS THEM

Once you have modeled the World Christian lifestyle and committed them to the Lord in your own heart, challenge them to lay their lives before the Lord and to offer themselves up as willing servants who say, "Here am I, Lord, send me."

KEY THREE: COMMUNITY

Encourage them to immerse themselves into a community with other World Christians. You will never consistently live out what you have learned if you don't live it out in community with other World Christians. Trying to live out a World Christian lifestyle in the middle of a bunch of worldly Christians is a recipe for lost vision and inaction. Red-hot coals don't stay aglow when you pull them away from other burning coals. Living the counter-cultural lifestyle of a World Christian is no different. Successfully exporting World Christians involves helping them land in a community where they are not considered "over-zealous nuts" because of their vision and lifestyle.

Dr. Ralph Winter, founder of the U.S. Center for World Mission, said, "If one hundred young people send a letter or an e-mail to the board stating, 'Tell me more about your work. I'm interested in the possibility of being a missionary,' only one out of a hundred ever goes."[73] What a tragedy! Fortunately, we have seen that when aspiring missionaries get in communities of other World Christians, nearly three quarters of them end up on the mission field. Wow! What a game-changer! Why not start a missional community specifically for "goers" (aspiring missionaries) in your church or ministry?[74]

KEY FOUR: COMMISSIONING

Play an active role in identifying well-prepared laborers and pointing them to strategic opportunities for impact. Following are some of the foundational questions and activities related to *Commissioning* those we lead.

PLAYING AN ACTIVE ROLE

When most of us think about commissioning someone, a common scenario comes to mind. A church member feels God may want him to serve on the mission field. He investigates different sending agencies and maybe talks with his pastor. After making his decision, he comes to the church and asks if they would commission him. This is what I call the "volunteer seeking the church's blessing" model. While there is nothing wrong with this model, we more frequently see a different one in Scripture. I call it the "faithful laborer gets recruited" model. In this model, a volunteer doesn't approach the church leadership; the church leadership approaches the faithful laborer. His future location of ministry is determined more by ministry leaders than by personal leadings. Here are a few examples.

> 2 Timothy 4:11 "*Get Mark* and bring him with you, because he is helpful to me in my ministry."

> Titus 1:5 "The reason *I left you* in Crete was that you might straighten out what was left unfinished and appoint elders in every town, as I directed you."

> Acts 15:27 "Therefore *we are sending* Judas and Silas to confirm by word of mouth what we are writing."

> Acts 15:40 "but *Paul chose* Silas…"

Do you think that the reason we are seeing so few laborers exported to the least-reached peoples is that God is not doing his part in answering our prayers? Or could it be that we are failing in our responsibility of actively identifying and selecting faithful laborers and challenging them to specific missions? A successful veteran missionary friend says that when he heard the voice of God telling him to go to the mission field, "It sounded a lot like the voice of my mission pastor." I have heard many people tell stories of how they ended up on the mission field as a result of a phone call from that same mission pastor telling them, "We need someone like you in country X."

I have met hundreds of people who are needlessly struggling with the question, "Where am I supposed to go?" all by themselves. They should be seeking out and involving their discipleship leaders, mission pastors, and church leaders in this decision. This is exactly what happened to Saul (later renamed Paul) and Barnabas.

> Now there were in the church at Antioch *prophets and teachers*, Barnabas, Simeon who was called Niger, Lucius of Cyrene, Manaen a lifelong friend of Herod the tetrarch, and Saul. While they were worshiping the Lord and fasting, the Holy Spirit said, "Set apart for me Barnabas and Saul for the work to which I have called them." Then after fasting and praying they laid their hands on them and sent them off. So, being sent out by the Holy Spirit, they went down to Seleucia, and from there they sailed to Cyprus. When they arrived at Salamis, they proclaimed the word of God in the synagogues of the Jews. *And they had John to assist them.* (Acts 13:1-5)

Were *Barnabas* and *Saul* told to set themselves apart? No, their group of leaders ("prophets and teachers") received the direction to set them apart. Certainly, Barnabas and Saul were a part of the group and process, but the call did not come to them alone. Once these men were clearly designated as mission team leaders by the church, they gathered and directed their team members, ministries, and locations. Notice in the last sentence that John was with them as their assistant. The Holy Spirit didn't mention his name. How did he end up on the team? The team leaders recruited him. Yes, he had a rough start at first, but later on he proved to be a very valuable team member.[75]

We see this pattern in the New Testament. God leads mission team members *through* mission team leaders in what they should do and where they should do it. Here is another example:

> And a vision appeared to *Paul* in the night: a man of Macedonia was standing there, urging him and saying, "Come over to Macedonia and help us." And when Paul had seen the vision, immediately we sought to go on into Macedonia, *concluding that God had called us* to preach the gospel to them. (Acts 16:9-10)

God gave the direction to Paul. What did the disciples conclude? That God was calling *them*. This was not a blind, unquestioning following. The passage seems to convey that they discussed it and came to a conclusion. Nevertheless, they didn't seem to expect that God would individually speak to each one of them. The Lord had spoken to their leader, and what he had heard was in line with what they knew of God's will.

We see this same pattern of God directing the comings and goings of disciple-makers through their leader in the following passages:

> *Paul wanted* Timothy to accompany him, and he took him… (Acts 16:3)

> As *I urged* you when I was going to Macedonia, remain at Ephesus… (1 Timothy 1:3)

> Do your best to *come* to me soon. (2 Timothy 4:9)

> Tychicus *I have sent* to Ephesus. (2 Timothy 4:12)

We must be less concerned about figuring out where we should serve and start submitting ourselves to trusted godly church and mission leaders for service. And to those of you who are leaders: when I look closely at Scripture, I don't get the feeling that we are overly injecting ourselves into the process of missionary guidance today. On the contrary, I sense that spiritual leaders are abdicating their God-given responsibility of speaking into the ministry placement and affairs of those they lead. We must take a more active role in exporting laborers.

BY WHAT AUTHORITY?

"How can I challenge others to go and live among the unreached when I have never done that?" I lived among Buddhists for many years, but I have never felt my experience qualifies me to challenge others to go. The authority by which I challenge people to consider giving their lives for the cause of Christ among the unreached does not originate from my personal history. It comes from the Word of God and my willingness to go *now*. No doubt, the Word of God alone is the authority, but I think it is a little easier to challenge people to go if I'm willing to go, right? I mean, how would it sound to say, "Hey, I think you should consider selling all of your possessions, leaving your family, and moving to Pakistan. I'm personally not willing to go, but I think you should be"?

How many times this past year have you challenged someone to consider moving to an unreached people group? We are Jesus' representatives on earth, right? He wants his church to go, right? Do you think he wants his representatives to speak on his behalf and exhort his disciples to go to all nations? If you are a World Christian and haven't challenged dozens of Christians in the last year to go to the unreached, is it because you haven't understood your role as his representative? Or is it because you personally haven't put your "yes" on the table and told Jesus that he is free to put it anywhere *he* wants on the map? Pray right now and repent of any inaction or an unsurrendered heart. Set a goal of how many people you will encourage to go to the unreached this year. I'll even provide a place for you to write that number.

> By God's grace, I will share God's heart for all nations and the need for laborers to go to the unreached with ________ people in the next year.

The reason there are still over 7,000 unreached people groups is not a shortage of laborers.[76] Two thousand years ago, there was a shortage of laborers in general. Today, we have approximately 1,000 churches for each remaining unreached people group.[77] We have enough laborers to finish the job. There are just way too many on one end of the log and not enough on the other. When I was told the story about the log to illustrate the gross imbalance of laborers in the world today, I was told that there were ten workers on one end and one on the other. If my missionary professor had used the actual numbers, he would have said that one end had 1,957 laborers and the other had one! The reason I moved my family back to the States after ten years among the unreached was not because I missed cheeseburgers. It was to yell at the top of my lungs, "We need some of you at the other end of the log!" Will you join me, by the authority of God's Word, in proclaiming to the church God's desire for all nations to know him? Start this week by sharing with just one person.

TO WHAT SHOULD WE CHALLENGE THEM?

Most of those we export will engage in ministry within their own people group. There is nothing less spiritual about that than crossing cultures into another group. The important thing is that *all* of us have a World Christian mindset and lifestyle that we pass along to those we lead. We should challenge everyone to "make it their ambition" to *see to it* that the gospel is preached where Christ is not known (Romans 15:20). Not everyone should go, but everyone should have the same goal no matter their role. Exporting is not just about sending goers to the unreached. Since Jesus wants every single believer to be fully engaged in fulfilling the Great Commission, we must mobilize everyone we disciple into *their most strategic role* in reaching all nations. If our focus is only on sending goers, we will never finish reaching all nations. To have the maximum impact on the nations, we need people to fill the roles of prayer team leaders, mobilizers, donors, trainers, legal advisors, international business consultants, local church mission committee members, welcomers of international students, and local disciple-makers. All of these roles are vital.

Long-term cross-cultural service should be the challenge many people are asked to consider. I am not against strategically planned short-term mission trips. They can do a lot of good. However, there has been an explosion in the number of these trips, and some of them do more harm than good. Possibly the greatest harm of all, though, is the inoculating effect on an individual believer's sense of mission. The believer hears of the need and thinks, "I need to do something." He goes on one or possibly a series of short-term trips and thinks, "I am doing what needs to be done." The honest truth is that we are not going to complete the job of reaching the 2.85 billion people who are beyond the church's reach with short-term workers. We need long-term laborers who will learn their languages, live in their neighborhoods, eat their food, have them in their homes, play with their children, cry with them when they hurt, and love them with all of their hearts.

There is no way to gain a depth of insight into a culture without living among them, learning their language, and building meaningful relationships. Long-term commitment has come to mean anything longer than a couple of weeks. In light of this, sending agencies have rolled out a plethora of two-month to two-year opportunities. This is the wrong approach. We must be honest with candidates and tell them plainly that it will take two years just to get comfortable in the language. True impact will more likely come in years three to ten.

BE HONEST ABOUT THE COST

We should not lessen the requirements on people who go. Instead, we must clearly state the difficulties in order to filter out those whose hearts are not fully committed.[78] It is said that when the explorer Ernest Shackleton needed men for his Antarctic exploration, he placed the following ad in the newspaper:

> Men wanted for hazardous journey. Low wages, bitter cold, long hours of complete darkness. Safe return doubtful. Honour and recognition in event of success.

It is reported that Shackleton had over 5,000 men respond to this ad.[79] Have we as today's mobilizers perhaps taken a wrong path in presenting less demanding opportunities to our recruits? Think of how Jesus recruited.

> As they were going along the road, someone said to him, "I will follow you wherever you go." And Jesus said to him, "Foxes have holes, and birds of the air have nests, but the Son of Man has nowhere to lay his head." To another he said, "Follow me." But he said, "Lord, let me first go and bury my father." And Jesus said to him, "Leave the dead to bury their own dead. But as for you, go and proclaim the kingdom of God." Yet another said, "I will follow you, Lord, but let me first say farewell to those at my home." Jesus said to him, "No one who puts his hand to the plow and looks back is fit for the kingdom of God." (Luke 9:57-62)

Jesus lets the requirements filter the men, not the men filter the requirements.

POINT TO THE REWARDS

Jesus spoke of both the reward and the persecution that await his kingdom workers:

> Jesus said, "Truly, I say to you, there is no one who has left house or brothers or sisters or mother or father or children or lands, for my sake and for the gospel, who will not receive a hundredfold now in this time, houses and brothers and sisters and mothers and children and lands, *with persecutions*, and in the age to come eternal life." (Mark 10:29-30, emphasis added)

I have found these words of Jesus to be true. I once left mother and father and brothers and sisters and houses to go to Thailand for the sake of the gospel. Today, if I were to go back to Thailand, I would find waiting for me mothers and fathers and brothers and sisters who would welcome me into their homes. One dear Thai sister has gone ahead of me to be with the Lord, and I will enjoy her friendship "in the age to come," just as Jesus promised. The treasure of these relationships and the influence I now have in their lives was not gained in a few weeks or months. You can't microwave disciples. We need to challenge people to go and stay where God plants them. Not until some arbitrary deadline, but until they have finished the work they set out to accomplish. The old axiom still holds true, "A missionary is someone who goes where they are *needed* but not wanted, and stays until they are *wanted* but not needed." No doubt, some missionaries hurt reproduction because they stay too long, but for most today, it is not staying long *enough* that kills their chances of having an enduring and exponentially multiplying impact.

Seeking the expansion of the kingdom of God here on earth may be very costly, but we will bear that cost joyfully when we consider what is gained by paying it. Notice this in the following parable:

> The kingdom of heaven is like treasure hidden in a field, which a man found and covered up. Then *in his joy he goes and sells all that he has* and buys that field. (Matthew 13:44)

We won't sweat what we have to give up when we focus on what we will gain. Temporal trinkets look like junk when we see that there is eternal treasure to be had!

HELP THEM GAIN AN ETERNAL PERSPECTIVE

If you don't have an eternal perspective, it is easy to worry too much about the near future. Certainly God cares about you and how you are doing now, but which is more important: how well you do for the next twenty years, or how well the Saudi Arabian people do for eternity? Christ came to earth and lived here even though it wouldn't end well for him. In the early years of missions in Africa, the missionaries sent their possessions there in coffins because they did not expect to live for more than a few years. They knew that they wouldn't "do well" there, but they went anyway because Christ is worth it. Paul didn't flee situations where it wouldn't go well for him. He saw them as part of his relationship with Christ and his service to the church. He embraced them joyfully. He says in Colossians, "Now I rejoice in my sufferings for your sake, and in my flesh I am filling up what is lacking in Christ's afflictions for the sake of his body, that is, the church..." (Colossians 1:24).

There is a story of an American missionary couple who returned to the United States by ship after several decades of faithful service in Africa. On board with them was President Teddy Roosevelt, who was returning from a game-hunting trip in Africa. He received V.I.P. treatment during the voyage while the missionary couple simply stood back and watched. Upon arrival in New York City, a crowd and a band had gathered to receive the politician. When he walked down the gangplank, music and loud applause greeted him as his motorcade whisked him away. Shanda Oakly writes about what happened next:

> Then quietly, with no fanfare, no attention, and no music, the missionary couple walked arm in arm down the gangplank, taking their first steps on American soil in over 30 years. After some silence, the husband turned to his wife and said, "Honey, it doesn't seem right after all these years that we would have nobody to greet us while that man got such a grand reception." The wife put her arms around her husband and gently reminded him, "But honey, we're not home yet."[80]

An eternal perspective makes all the difference!

CONSTANTLY SPEAK OF SERVING GOD AS A PRIVILEGE

God does not *need* us. He could make stones rise up and preach the gospel (Luke 19:40) or enable animals to share his message (Numbers 22:28-30). God *allows* us to work alongside him in his great mission of bringing the nations to himself. When I was a kid, my father would fix our cars and lawnmowers himself. If he was out in the garage on a Saturday morning fixing something, there was a good chance I was out there too, "helping" him. Did he need my assistance? No. In fact, I'm sure I probably slowed things down. But he loved me, and it was good for my growth and development to work alongside him, so he allowed it. We are not doing God a favor when we serve him. He *allows* us to do it for our own good and for the blessing that comes from joining him. Let your disciples hear you give thanks to the

Lord frequently for the privilege of serving him. Only a grateful attitude will lead to longevity in ministry.

While it is true that God doesn't need us, it is also true that he has chosen to spread his gospel to the ends of the earth through us. He has good works prepared in advance that he wants us to do, and the world is waiting. J. Oswald Sanders, author and former director of the China Inland Mission (now Overseas Missionary Fellowship), tells the story of the time he visited one of their missionaries in the Philippines. While there, the first person to trust Christ in a particular village was baptized. The new believer was an elderly grandmother. The missionary stood with her in the river and began asking her some questions before immersing her in the water. First he asked, "Grandmother, do you believe that Jesus is the Son of God?" She replied, "Yes." Then he asked her if she believed that he died for her sins. She again replied, "Yes." Next he asked if she believed she would spend eternity with God in heaven. Once more she replied, "Yes." As he began to ask a fourth question she became frustrated with him and exclaimed, "Of course I believe. And I would have believed sooner if you would have come sooner!" Do you think God may have prepared a people to whom he wants you to mobilize your disciples, or even go yourself? I do. Sadly, most of us feel so unprepared and unqualified that we will not attempt the great things God wants us to do. Read on to get beyond this feeling and learn how to unleash others for exponential impact.

THE MULTIPLICATION CYCLE

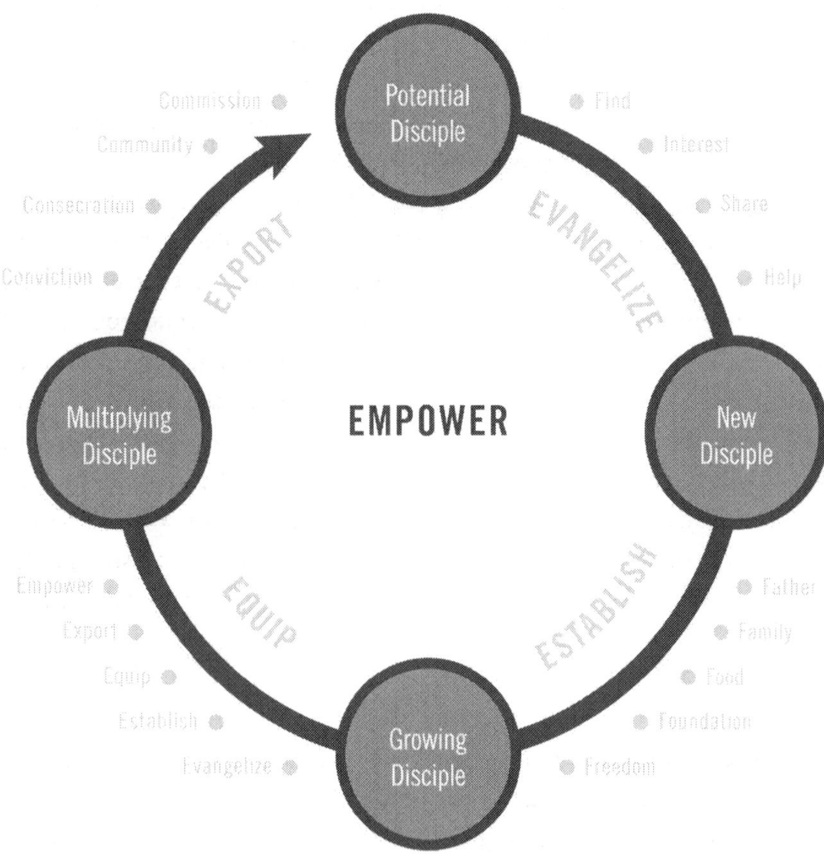

CHAPTER 10

YOU CAN!

[EMPOWERING]

In the circus, baby elephants are kept from wandering off by being chained to a stake in the ground. When they are small, the stake is sufficient to hold them, and they learn through repeated attempts of tugging on it that they can't get free. As they grow, though, the stake becomes inadequate to hold them back. Yet the full-grown elephants don't pull it up and walk off. Why? Because they believe the lie that they can't do it. That lie keeps them in bondage and from running free. What about people? Is it possible for someone to be fully capable of doing something and yet not even try because they believe they can't do it? Of course it is. The important question is, what about you? Are there things God has perfectly created and gifted you to do that you aren't even attempting because you believe you can't or shouldn't try them? What about the people you are discipling? Are they failing to attempt some aspect of ministry because they believe they aren't capable of it or that they need someone's blessing first? Could hearing an *empowering* truth from you be just what they need to break free from the constraining lie and into exponential impact? After all, didn't Jesus say "the truth will set you free"?[81]

SATAN'S LIES

Satan does not want you or the people you are discipling to attempt great things with God. He will use every lie available to him to keep you tied to the stake. If persuading you to believe you can't do something is too overt, he will simply use a more subtle strategy. This involves making you think you must wait until sometime in the future before you attempt what God is prompting you to do. The inaction created by the "wait" lie is as crippling as that of the "You can't do it" lie. You know the type of lies I am talking about. They are very familiar.

- You don't know enough. You can't share the gospel yet.
- You still have too much sin in your life. You are not ready to disciple someone else.
- You've blown it. You've gone too far. He can't use you anymore.
- You're too young. You need to wait until you are older.
- You're too old. It's too late to start now. What's the point at this age?
- You don't have time. Next year will be better.
- You don't have the credentials. You're not qualified. People won't follow you.
- You still need someone to disciple you. After you have grown more, then you can disciple others.
- You don't have "a life worth emulating." You will just multiply your weaknesses.
- Don't even think about starting a church. You're not qualified, and it requires a lot of money.

As you know, Satan is the author of lies.[82] However, he sure gets a lot of help from people, doesn't he? The world and the church are full of well-meaning people who will tell you "You can't" when that's just not true. Yet they believe it is true and therefore pass the lie along with vigor to others in an attempt to be helpful. Unfortunately, if no one questions the validity of a statement, the lie will live on, keeping people staked and even spreading to others.

I saw this happen on a golf course in Thailand. The retreat center where we were staying was in a mountainous area, and the golf course was pretty hilly. About halfway through our round, we came to a long par-three hole. As we were selecting clubs to use to tee off, our caddies informed us that there was an optical illusion in play with this hole. They said that although the green looked significantly lower than the tee, it was actually quite a bit higher. There was a deep valley in between the two that they said helped trick the eye. When I took a look, I told my caddy that there was no way the green was higher than the tee. At this point, the other three caddies jumped in and adamantly tried to convince me that my eyes were being fooled. Even though it looked like I would be hitting downhill, I would actually be hitting uphill. It was clear that they were all convinced what they were telling me was true. After reaching the green and looking back to the tee, I was still unconvinced. Then I had an idea. I had received a handheld GPS for my birthday and brought it along on the trip. I decided I would throw it in the golf bag and use it to read the altitude of both the tee and the green the next afternoon. When I did, it confirmed that my eyes and the eyes of everyone else who played that hole were right. The tee was significantly higher than the green.

What had happened? Here is my theory: Sometime in the past, someone (probably a weak golfer who couldn't reach the green) came up with the notion that the green was higher than the tee. The golfer convinced the caddy it was true. That caddy told some other caddies, and the lie spread and became more firmly believed over time as more and more people told it as fact. However it came about, one thing is for sure—a bunch of people were believing and spreading a lie.

Could the church do the same thing? Is it possible that we believe some limiting lies about ministry and pass them on to others? Maybe they have become so firmly established among us that we don't even question them anymore. Don't you wish we had a GPS to settle issues? The good news is that we do have one: God's infallible Word.

JESUS OUR MODEL

It would be easy to fill this whole chapter with observations of how Jesus *empowered* his disciples. Let's look briefly at how he **A.R.M.**ed (**A**uthority, **R**esources and **M**otivation) them for ministry.

AUTHORITY

In Luke 10, Jesus gives seventy-two of his followers the responsibility to go out and preach the gospel and heal the sick in the places where he was about to go. He did not give them the responsibility without authority, though. In verse 19, he says, "Behold, I have given you authority…" Jesus did not give the responsibility and corresponding authority only to the twelve apostles. He empowered all seventy-two. It is not a select few "Super Christians" who must take responsibility for making disciples and forming churches. Nor is the authority limited to a small band of the elite. The one who has "all authority on heaven and earth" has given it to all of his followers to multiply his church in all nations.[83]

RESOURCES

It is frustrating to be given a heavy responsibility and little or no resources to get the job done. I have been in that situation before, and it felt like I was asked to make bricks without being given any straw! Jesus didn't operate that way. He let his disciples know that if they needed something, they could call on him. He would get them the needed resources, partnership or wisdom they lacked.[84] Jesus didn't dump a responsibility on them and then disappear. He committed to resource them as needed.

MOTIVATION

Nothing motivates like big vision. Jesus was constantly casting a vision for his followers. He told them they were a part of something big. Something eternal. He made it personal with them. He assured them that not only were they involved in something big, but they would be able to make a big impact by being a part of it. In fact, they would actually do greater works than he was doing.[85]

If nothing motivates like vision, nothing demotivates like failure. When you attempt something and fail, you can easily lose your confidence and feel like throwing in the towel. The wise disciple-maker will follow Jesus' model of not just helping people understand why they failed, but also encouraging them with what God can do through them. Notice how Jesus does both:

> Then the disciples came to Jesus privately and said, "Why could we not cast it out?" He said to them, "Because of your little faith. For truly, I say to you, if you have faith like a grain of mustard seed, you will say to this mountain, 'Move from here to there,' and it will move, and nothing will be impossible for you." (Matthew 17:19-21)

At a time when they were probably feeling particularly defeated and powerless, it must have been extremely encouraging and motivating to hear, "Nothing will be impossible for you."

A CONTEMPORARY ROLE MODEL

When I think of a role model for equipping and empowering people for ministry, I think of my former pastor Frank Barker. He is a gifted Bible expositor and planted a church that grew to over 4,000 members under his leadership. However, his greatest contribution to the kingdom is arguably not what *he* has done, but what he has empowered *others* to do. When members of his church (and many people who were not members) approached him with a vision God had laid on their hearts, his typical response was, "Wonderful, how can I help?" What amazes me is that he actually meant it. Even though he pastored a large church, he found time to help his members launch *their* ministries. He could have stayed busy flying all over the world teaching, but he saw his job as an equipper and "empowerer" of "the saints to do the work of the ministry."[86] He highly valued helping *others* succeed at disciple-making. In his mind, his church did not exist to enable him to minister. He existed to help *them* minister. Although he could have spent most of his time speaking to large crowds, Frank didn't think it poor stewardship of his time to help just one of his members start a personal ministry. He viewed it as an investment that would multiply. Indeed it did.

The result of this *empowering others* approach to ministry is that there are now thriving and expanding ministries that reach far beyond one local church—college ministries, business leader's ministries, dance ministries, high school ministries, church planting ministries, urban ministries, and seminary ministries. All of these came about not because of Frank's giftedness, but because of his willingness to empower others.

Long before Frank, though, we saw this same empowering approach practiced by Barnabas. He took Saul (Paul) under his wing and helped him get started in ministry when others wouldn't. He allowed Paul to teach with him and even let him do most of the speaking.[87] Could it be that our goal should not be to build a successful ministry, but to help others build theirs? Imagine what could happen if you made empowering others the focus of your ministry!

Empowering is not a stage in the disciple-making cycle. It must happen throughout the whole process. That's why you find it at the center of my diagram entitled The Multiplication Cycle at the beginning of this chapter.

The lies that Satan will tell believers at different stages of their growth and ministry will change, so we need to vary our empowering message and actions accordingly. Let's examine some of the common lies Satan tells us at different stages of our discipleship journey, beginning with potential disciples and working our way through to mobilized disciples.

EMPOWERING POTENTIAL DISCIPLES

Lie from Satan: Your life won't make a difference in the world. Live for yourself.

Truth from Christ: Your life can impact the world and eternity, just like the early disciples did.

These men who have turned the world upside down have come here also… (Acts 17:6)

Years ago, my friend Mike Hearon taught me about empowering potential disciples. Mike would talk to lost students about how God could use their lives to impact the world and eternity. My first reaction was, "Why are you talking with people who are going to hell about how God could multiply their lives? They need to hear the gospel!" Mike understood that the gospel isn't merely Jesus helping you escape hell. He can help you escape a meaningless existence on earth, too. That's good news and an important part of the gospel! We talked in Chapter Six about the importance of creating interest as we evangelize. Mike had tuned into the fact that young men and women have a God-given desire to live a life of significance. This is especially true of young adults who are considering how they want to spend their lives. The message that there is more to life than getting up, going to work, then coming home to watch television, is encouraging. We must empower potential disciples to have a new vision for their lives. In the Garden of Eden before the fall, Adam not only had a relationship with God, but he also had work to do. Jesus not only calls us into a relationship with him, but he also calls us to a task. "Follow me and I will make you fishers of men" (Matthew 4:19). Can you think of some potential disciples that you can share this good news with today?

EMPOWERING NEW DISCIPLES

Lie from Satan: You don't know enough yet to share your faith with others.

Truth from Christ: I will be with you and help you.

> When they deliver you over, do not be anxious how you are to speak or what you are to say, for what you are to say will be given to you in that hour. For it is not you who speak, but the Spirit of your Father speaking through you. (Matthew 10:19-20)

We need to encourage new Christians to start sharing their faith immediately. Our research found that the key to winning a lot of people to Christ was not having more training, but sharing more frequently. Since new Christians usually have a lot more lost friends than people who have been Christians longer, they are actually in a better position to lead people to Christ.

EMPOWERING NEW BELIEVERS TO WITNESS FOR CHRIST

The myth that growth in Christ must precede evangelism is clearly that—a myth. Listen to a description of the early days of Paul's (then Saul's) ministry:

> For some days he was with the disciples at Damascus. And *immediately he proclaimed Jesus* in the synagogues, saying, "He is the Son of God." And all who heard him were amazed and said, "Is not this the man who made havoc in Jerusalem of those who called upon this name? And has he not come here for this purpose, to bring them bound before the chief priests?" But *Saul increased all the more in strength*, and confounded the Jews who lived in Damascus by proving that Jesus was the Christ. (Acts 9:19-22)

He began sharing Christ after being a follower for only a few days. Which came first, proclamation or growth? We need to empower new believers with the truth that they can and should immediately be witnesses for Christ. And we should encourage them with the reality that growth results from witnessing, not the other way around.[88]

What about someone who doesn't have formal Bible training? What if they even have a bad reputation in the community? Could they begin witnessing immediately after coming to Christ and be effective? Absolutely. Look what happened when an adulteress became an immediate witness: "Many Samaritans from that town believed in him because of the woman's testimony, 'He told me all that I ever did.'" (John 4:39)

Jesus doesn't just allow new believers to begin witnessing. He *desires* it! He commanded a man who had just been freed from demons to go share his testimony.

> As he was getting into the boat, the man who had been possessed with demons begged him that he might be with him. And he did not permit him but said to him, "Go home to your friends and tell them how much the Lord has done for you, and how he has had mercy on you." And he went away and began to proclaim in the Decapolis how much Jesus had done for him, and everyone marveled. (Mark 5:18-20)

The man's natural desire was to be with Jesus. He even begged Jesus to allow him to accompany him. He probably felt that he needed to experience a time of further healing from his past before he could minister to others. Yet Jesus empowered him with the truth that he could begin to have an impact immediately. And he did! When he shared, the text says, "everyone marveled."

REASONS TO EMPOWER NEW BELIEVERS TO WITNESS

There are great benefits that come to the hearts and minds of new believers as a result of being engaged in sharing their new faith. In his book *Dedication and Leadership,* Douglas Hyde, who left the Communist Party after coming to Christ, tells how the Party trained new recruits. Notice the parallels to new Christians and evangelism.

> The instruction of the new Party member does not normally begin immediately after he joins. Quite deliberately, and with good reason, the Party sends its new members, whenever possible, into some form of public activity before instruction begins. More specifically, it is designed to commit the recruit publicly to Communism.

Quite often this will take the form of being sent out to stand at the side of the street or in some public place selling Communist papers, periodicals or pamphlets. This may appear to be a very simple, somewhat low-grade form of activity. It is in fact of profound psychological significance. For the new recruit, still having to adjust his mind to the thought that he is now a Communist (and he knows that for a large section of the public the very name is a dirty word), this is something very significant indeed. He is making a public witness for the cause which he is now making his own.

...he sees people looking at him with suspicion or even hatred. Then, perhaps, someone breaks from the crowd and starts abusing him... But the crowd that begins to gather is a mixed one. He now finds himself having to deal with more rational objections to his Communism. This makes him draw deeply upon such small resources as he has got in the way of knowledge of current events, of the past, present and future of Communism, of the Party's policies, philosophy, the activities of its leaders. His inclination is to take to his heels and bolt. It requires another act of moral courage to remain in a fight for which, he by now realizes, he is not fully equipped. And moral courage is not a bad starting-point for future action.

The questions continue. 'Why did you join the Communist Party? 'You don't look like a bad sort of fellow, so how can you possibly join such a party when you know what Russia did in Hungary?' 'Why did Joe Stalin conclude a pact with Hitler?' 'If you're a Communist, you must be an atheist. How can anyone but a fool be an atheist today?' And so it goes on.

He gives such answers as he can. When it is all over, he heaves a sigh of relief, leaves his pitch and takes away his bundle of unsold papers. But he also takes away the knowledge that he has not got all the answers to the questions he is likely to be asked as a Communist. He is conscious now that he knows less than he thought he did. Quite probably he is dissatisfied with himself. He would dearly have loved to put up a tremendous fight for his new-found faith, taking on and defeat-

> ing, or converting, all comers. He has done nothing of the sort. But he has learned his own inadequacy. This, one might say, is the beginning of wisdom.
>
> Those who sent him into this form of activity did not expect him to have all the answers. He has let down neither the Party nor himself. In the process he has learned a good deal. When he next takes up his stand at the side of the road, he will come determined to do better. Most probably, he has been reading Communist papers in a different way, looking for the answers to the questions he was asked last time. Gathering shot and shell in readiness for the next fight. This is when he really begins to learn—and the desire to learn now comes from within himself. He is seeking to make himself more adequate, more worthy of the Party, better able to serve the cause. And his newfound thirst for knowledge about Communism, the sense of urgency which he feels as he reads and tries to understand the Communist books and papers has grown from action. Theory and action—those apparent opposites—have found a unity in his mind and in his experience.[89]

The Communists are not the only ones who have found great benefit in the practice of getting new followers to share their beliefs immediately. Church planting movements around the world have discovered this principle. The following is an excerpt from an interview with veteran missionary Curtis Sergeant about his team's ministry practices, which led to a great multiplication of disciples and churches. Notice how they cast vision and empowered new believers to both dream big and act immediately.

> How quickly were new believers expected to share their faith and even plant churches? Immediately! As soon as someone came to Christ, Sergeant or one of his team members would say the following: "It is a great blessing to lead someone else to Christ. It is an even greater blessing to start a church. It is the greatest blessing to train others to start churches. I want you to have the greatest blessing, but let's start with great blessing." So together, they would make a list of 100 friends and begin to role-play sharing the Gospel with five friends. Then they would pray and go and share with their five friends right away. After that new be-

> liever came to Christ, he or she would repeat the same phrases. Many wouldn't really know how to plant a church yet, but they would learn over time as one duckling follows the other. One disciples another who may be only one step behind.[90]

EMPOWERING WITH THE PROMISES OF CHRIST

We must empower new believers for evangelism by sharing with them the promises of Christ—how he will be with them and give them the words they need. It is encouraging for them to hear stories of times when Christ clearly assisted an inadequate witness to get the job done. One of my favorite stories to share is about a girl named Rachel who went to Thailand with us on a short-term trip. One evening, our group was walking through a street market. Rachel and some of her friends saw an elderly, crippled lady sitting on the street corner begging. The girls felt led to stop and pray for the woman. Rachel had been learning a little of the Thai language and used it to ask the lady if she could pray for her. Afterwards Rachel felt a burden to share the gospel with the woman and attempted to in her broken Thai. Frustrated with her inability, Rachel silently prayed to God for help. Immediately, a Thai woman came out of the masses streaming by and asked, "Weren't you girls at my church last Sunday?" Rachel said yes and that she was now trying to share the gospel with this woman and needed help. The Thai believer jumped in and helped share Christ.

To realize what an answer to prayer this was, one needs to understand the context. Bangkok has over eight million inhabitants living in a six hundred square mile area. The market where the girls were is not close to the church where they met. At that time, Rachel had only met a few dozen believers. So what are the chances that she would coincidentally bump into one of the few believers she had met in Bangkok's millions, at just the right location in the six hundred square mile city, and at the exact second that week when she prayed and asked for help? Stories like Rachel's can empower those we disciple with the truth that if they will step out in faith, God will deliver.

Before we move on, maybe you need to let the following truth marinate in your own heart: *The most effective disciple-makers aren't the ones who are the best trained. They are the ones who share with the most people!* Are you ready to chuck the fear and start sharing with everybody?

> *Lie from Satan:* You are not yet capable to start your own disciple-making team.
>
> *Truth from Christ:* Your competence comes from God.
>
> Not that we are competent in ourselves to claim anything for ourselves, but our competence comes from God. He has made us competent as ministers of a new covenant…(2 Corinthians 3:5-6)

Satan would love for you to delay starting your own cell group (disciple-making team). He knows that the longer you wait, the less likely you are to ever do it. And when you finally do start, it will take longer to multiply because you will have less contact with lost people. Joel Comiskey did research on cell group multiplication. He found a correlation between the length of time someone has been saved and how long it takes them to multiply their group.[91] The longer someone is a believer, the longer it takes them to multiply their cell group. The sooner we get people laboring, the better.

I am a teacher and trainer at heart, and I believe that disciples benefit from solid Bible teaching and discipling. Because of that, I have to remind myself that it is rarely advisable to require people to frontload all of their training. The best training comes while you're on the job, and it comes when you actually need it. Not before. The most teachable and trainable people are usually those who are already in the battle. Neil Cole speaks of the importance of not holding converts back from laboring in his book *Organic Church*:

> We have made a terrible mistake by separating the convert from the worker. They are not two, but one. Each new convert is a new worker. We sin when we expect the convert to wait a while, any time at all, to become a worker. Each new convert is a worker—immediately…
>
> We are not to wait for a time as though the new convert is lacking anything. What are they missing? They are sealed in the Holy Spirit. They gain immediate and constant access to Almighty God. They have the power of the Scriptures available. They inherit all that comes with being a child of God. They are washed clean of all sins and blights against heaven. Why do we think they need something more from us? What

> arrogance it is for us to add to all God has given them the need for our training! What blasphemy it is for us to tell people that they are not ready to be a worker until they have been through our curriculum![92]

Still not sure you are ready to start discipling someone? Curtis Sergeant, missionary trainer, saw firsthand how God can multiply disciples and churches through unlikely people. He shares the following words of encouragement in an interview about church planting movements and specifically addresses the concern that rapidly multiplying churches may not have adequate leadership.

> **Interviewer:** What about leadership, with so few people formally trained, or even having been Christians very long?
>
> **Sergeant:** When you see a family of ducks crossing the road, only the first duckling is following the mother. The rest are following the duckling in front of them. None of us has achieved the full measure of the stature of Christ. Every one is mature enough to be a leader of another duckling. "Follow me as I follow Christ." Each of us, including a brand new follower, is ready and responsible to lead others to Christ. Everything we receive, we have an obligation to pass on to others."[93]

EMPOWERING GROWING DISCIPLES

Lie from Satan: You can't plant a church. You don't have what it takes.

Truth from Christ: You can do all things through Christ who strengthens you.

> I can do all things through him who strengthens me. (Philippians 4:13)

If we are going to see the world reached for Christ, we must plant millions of new churches. To keep that from happening, Satan wants Christians to believe that they can't plant a church unless they have a whole list of things that simply aren't required by God. This list includes a seminary degree, money, a building, the blessing of some church body, a minimum age, a particular temperament type, a certain spiritual gift, and a high capacity to juggle responsibilities and get things done. None of the items on this list are bad, and all could be helpful in planting a new church. However, we must break free from the lie that any of them are actually *required* to plant a new church. This freedom is happening in many places around the world, and where it is, the church is multiplying and expanding at staggering rates.[94]

REDEFINING CHURCH

One of the keys to empowering people to plant churches and unleash church planting movements is to strip away all cultural and historical baggage from our definition of church. When we decide to add nothing more to our definition of church than the New Testament requires, we end up with a very simple and uncomplicated model of church that can replicate rapidly. Our tendency, though, is to make things bigger and more complex than they have to be. Thinking that bigger is better, we build what many have called "elephant churches" that are slow and hard to reproduce. We don't need to kill elephant churches (I attend one), but we do need to affirm that small "rabbit churches" are equally valid forms of church.

Consider the following: Elephants don't reach sexual maturity until they are around fifteen, and they may not actually reproduce until years later. Additionally, females are only fertile four times a year. Pregnancy lasts twenty-two months and only produces one calf. Intervals between calves are approximately four to five years. Rabbits, on the other hand, reach sexual maturity at four months and are almost continually fertile. Gestation takes only one month and yields an average of seven babies. If you locked two elephants in a room and came back three years later, you would find up to three elephants. If you did the same with two rabbits, there could be 476 million! Don't try this at home.

So what might a rabbit church look like? One model that has proven healthy and highly reproducible is the POUCH church. POUCH stands for:

Participative Bible study and worship,
Obedience as the mark of success for every believer and church,
Unpaid and multiple leaders in each church,
Cell groups of ten to twenty believers meeting in
Homes or storefronts.[95]

When trying to envision what a POUCH church is like, just think about the church in the book of Acts and 1 Corinthians 14:26-33. What we find in these Scriptures are relatively small, interactive groups of ordinary people following hard after Jesus. As they live and minister in simple community, they multiply, and the kingdom advances![96]

DEBUNKING SATAN'S LIES ABOUT CHURCH

Believing something is required beyond what the Scriptures say is necessary can keep disciple-makers from planting new churches. Therefore, we must expose the fallacies in Satan's lies like those that follow.

"YOU MUST HAVE A SEMINARY DEGREE TO LEAD A CHURCH."

This lie is not universally believed around the world. However, one of the more difficult places to free believers from extra-biblical expectations of church leadership has been North America. J.D. Payne, Pastor for Church Multiplication at The Church at Brook Hills in Alabama, has done extensive research on church planting. He asserts:

> …many North American churches have a very unhealthy understanding of church leadership. In most cases, we define leadership in terms of academic achievements and popularity, instead of defining leadership according to the biblical guidelines; we tend to define leadership in a very narrow and exclusive sense. Ask yourself, how many of the biblical guidelines for overseers are related to academic achievement, including the ability to teach and exhort from the Scriptures? How many of the qualifications for leadership are related to character, moral, ethical, and familial areas… An unhealthy understanding of leadership hinders the possibility of church multiplication.[97]

Is a seminary degree helpful? If it is from a theologically solid school, it usually is. Neither Dr. Payne nor I would discourage pursuing seminary training. However, the biblical requirements for leading a church do not include an academic degree. Some of the best seminary students I have ever taught were the ones who were *already* pastoring churches. They were more motivated and had better questions than those not already ministering. I'm glad they didn't wait to graduate before they started leading! Certainly we need more seminary-trained pastors. However, for the kingdom to keep pressing forward, we must have an unhindered stream of workers join the ranks of the hundreds of thousands of non-seminary trained pastors in the world.

Not having a degree should not stop any biblically qualified person from starting or leading a church.[98] Having a degree doesn't mean that you won't twist the Scriptures. Some of the most dangerous Scripture-twisters I know of have PhDs. I also know a lot of non-seminary trained pastors who faithfully and accurately preach the Word week in and week out. If your situation allows you to obtain a degree, go for it. If not, please don't let that stop you from planting churches or empowering others to do so.

"YOU MUST HAVE MONEY TO PLANT A CHURCH."

I read an encouraging book last year about multiplying churches. The early chapters were filled with great truths about how God can use anyone to start and multiply churches. Then, near the end of the book, the author suddenly gave a list of things needed to start a new church that included a huge budget, lots of sound equipment, a talented group of musicians, and a large group of people for a launch team. I've got to believe that this list disempowered and sucked the vision out of most aspiring church planters who read it. I'm glad the apostle Paul didn't believe this! If he did, he would have never started any churches.

You don't need *any* money if you have a multiplication philosophy of ministry. Just start meeting with a few people as a disciple-making team, and watch what God does! No money is required if you are willing to *grow* into ministry. This model allows for the multiplication of churches that is not restrained by dependence on outside resources.

"YOU MUST HAVE A BUILDING TO PLANT A CHURCH."

The Kui people live in the southern part of the state of Orissa in India. A recent report showed that they were starting a new church about every twenty-four hours, meeting in open courtyards. The church is also growing rapidly among the Maasai in East Africa. Most of their churches gather under acacia trees, the traditional meeting places for Maasai councils.[99] Don't tell the Kui or Maasai that they must have a building to start a new church. They will not agree.

Please don't believe the lie that brick and mortar will somehow make a church more permanent. Right now across Europe, Muslims are converting church buildings into mosques. At least 10,000 churches have been closed in Britain alone since 1960, and another 4,000 are set to close by 2020.[100] Enduring churches come from successful disciple-making, not from buildings.

"YOU MUST HAVE SOMEONE ELSE'S BLESSING TO PLANT A CHURCH."

Church history shows us that well-meaning men frequently set up hierarchical structures that they hope will protect the church and its doctrines. Interestingly, those which are the most hierarchically structured are generally those which have wandered the farthest from the Bible.

In his book, *The Spontaneous Expansion of the Church: And Causes that Hinder It,* Roland Allen makes a case for empowering believers to start and multiply churches without the approval of governing bodies, especially foreign ones. The forward itself is very helpful. It states:

> He [Allen] argues that from the moment the first group of converts appears they must be equipped fully with all spiritual authority so that they may multiply themselves. This he claims would open the way to unlimited expansion, and he cites as a case in point the story of the Church in Madagascar. For twenty-five years all missionaries were driven from this island, and the Christian community passed through a period of bitter persecution. At the end of this quarter of a century missionaries were allowed to return. They found that, instead of the Church having died out for lack of western help and supervision, it had grown and multiplied tenfold.
>
> Basing his argument on apostolic practice, he believes that the present method of appointing foreign Bishops, superintending missionaries and western organization is the road to sterility, not growth. If groups of native Christians have only a partial ministry and have to wait for foreign funds to open mission stations, they are in a bondage that ultimately leads to revolt and resentment.[101]

I do believe that a properly administered ordination process can provide a healthy set of checks and balances in a church multiplication movement.

However, many times in church history, well-intentioned believers have withheld their blessing on someone's pursuit of ministry in light of some cultural bias or man-made tradition. One example of this is the concept of age.

"YOU ARE TOO YOUNG TO PLANT OR LEAD A CHURCH."

"Let no one despise you for your youth, but set the believers an example in speech, in conduct, in love, in faith, in purity" (1 Timothy 4:12). Paul tells Timothy that he can overcome being looked down on because of his youth if he will show maturity in the way he lives. Does it really work? Consider this:

- In October of 1517, God used a thirty-three-year-old monk named *Martin Luther* to start what became known as the Protestant Reformation.
- *John Wesley* was only twenty-six when he started his "holy clubs," sparking revival on England's campuses.
- One of the most influential theological works in the history of the Church, *John Calvin's Institutes of the Christian Religion*, was written by a young man in his early twenties.
- *George Whitfield* was twenty when he joined one of Wesley's holy clubs and twenty-five during his first mission trip to America in 1739 where he preached to open air crowds as large as 30,000 people.
- *William Carey* was an illiterate cobbler until he was saved as a teenager. He immediately tacked a world map to his cobbler's bench and began to educate himself. Carey eventually produced more than 200,000 Bibles and tracts in forty different languages. In 1792, Carey was thirty-one when he birthed the modern mission movement.
- *Charles Spurgeon*, the greatest preacher of the nineteenth century, started preaching at sixteen and attracted large crowds. By age thirty, he had built and filled the 5,000-seat Metropolitan Tabernacle in London.
- *William Booth*, founder of the Salvation Army, started preaching in the slums of London while still a teenager.
- In 1844, *George Williams*, a twenty-three-year-old businessman, started the Young Men's Christian Association (YMCA) as an evangelistic outreach to businessmen.

- In 1722, *Count Ludwig von Zinzendorf* founded a Christian community dedicated to prayer and world missions at age twenty-two. Its followers eventually became known as the Moravians. They had a prayer chain that lasted 100 years, and their mission work spanned the globe.
- *George Müller* was saved at twenty and founded the world-famous Bristol Orphanage ten years later.
- At the age of twenty-one, *Jonathan Edwards* preached the sermon that sparked the "Great Awakening," bringing thousands to a living faith in Christ and laying the spiritual foundation for what would become the United States of America.[102]

And the list keeps going.

It is not just men whom God has used at an early age. If we started listing women like Grace Wilder, who quietly helped launch the Student Volunteer Movement while she was still a college student, or Amy Carmichael, who started impacting countless lives when she was just in her early twenties, we could fill volumes. Male or female, young or old, God will use you if you will ask him to and then step out in faith. Think you're too young? Think again!

What about grey-haired readers? I want to encourage you with what a seventy-eight-year-old man told me. He said the Holy Spirit convicted him two years earlier that he was wasting his life playing golf every day. Soon after that, he decided to go on a mission trip with his church. He eventually began leading trips and training leaders. Consider also the 101-year-old disciple-maker Jim Downing. He is still at it with no plan of quitting that I can see. You're never too old!

"YOU DON'T HAVE THE RIGHT TEMPERAMENT OR GIFTS TO PLANT OR LEAD A CHURCH."

It does take a certain gift set to lead big and complex elephant churches. This is not true with simple rabbit churches. There is no correlation between temperament or spiritual gift type and frequency of multiplication.[103] We have made church planting something only for the super talented, like playing for the Yankees. We need to make it more like a Monday night softball game where everyone can play.[104]

EMPOWERING MULTIPLYING DISCIPLES

There are many lies that Satan tells a multiplying disciple whom you are trying to empower. We will look briefly at just three. The first is common to anyone considering a move (a graduating senior from college, for example), and the next two are for those who are considering moving into ministry to the unreached.

> *Lie from Satan:* You can have a ministry anywhere. Just find the best job you can and *then* figure out the ministry piece.
>
> *Truth from Christ:* Seek God's kingdom first, and he will provide what you need.
>
> But seek first the kingdom of God and his righteousness, and all these things will be added to you. (Matthew 6:33)

Let vision, not provision, drive your decisions. The Word of God points to the need for believers to be a part of a disciple-making team. However, year after year, I see people make decisions to move to locations where there is no disciple-making team or church for them to join. You can find believers almost anywhere with whom you can fellowship. Finding people who truly value and practice laboring in the harvest together is much harder. *The team is more important than the ballpark.* Get yourself on a team with people who will help each other multiply and trust God for provision to follow.

For those who are considering moving to some unreached area of the world, the following lies need to be addressed.

> *Lie from Satan:* You can't learn a language.
>
> *Truth from Christ:* God's grace is sufficient in weakness.
>
> But he said to me, "My grace is sufficient for you, for my power is made perfect in weakness." (2 Corinthians 12:9)

I had a horrible time with college French. The experience convinced me that if I was ever going to be a missionary, I needed to go somewhere they spoke English. Fortunately, after college I learned a little about what it really takes to learn a language. As I did, I began to realize that my experience of learning a language on the mission field would be completely different than what I experienced in the college classroom. In college, I lacked important things like real motivation to study and an opportunity to practice daily what I was learning. No one I know has ever left the field because they couldn't learn the language. You can do it!

> *Lie from Satan:* Support raising is begging, and you probably wouldn't reach your goal anyway.
>
> *Truth from Christ:* The laborer is worth his wage, and God will provide for your needs.
>
> For the Scripture says, "You shall not muzzle an ox when it treads out the grain," and, "The laborer deserves his wages." (1 Timothy 5:18)
>
> And my God will supply every need of yours according to his riches in glory in Christ Jesus. (Philippians 4:19)

God's finger will not point where his hand will not provide. As Hudson Taylor said, "God's work done in God's way will never lack God's supply."[105] There are literally thousands of people in the world who raise their personal support and would have it no other way. They have discovered the blessing of living by faith and of developing a team of partners who pray for and invest in their ministries.[106]

EMPOWERING MOBILIZED DISCIPLES

Certainly by the time someone gets to the point of being a mobilized disciple, he or she has grown beyond believing all of Satan's lies mentioned thus far, right? To test that theory, I wrote over fifteen full-time Christian workers who would fall into the category of mobilized disciples. I asked them, "What is the biggest lie Satan tells you to keep you from attempting something great for God or to get you to quit trying?" Their responses are as follows:

LIES FROM SATAN:

1. I don't know enough.
2. I fear failure and man—what people think about me.
3. I fear that I might fail! I won't have enough time to do something good enough.
4. My attempts will always fall short.
5. What I offer is not good enough.
6. I don't have enough skills or experience.
7. I'm not doing enough, or the things I am doing, I'm not doing well enough.
8. Maybe I don't have what it takes.
9. I'm not good enough yet.
10. God won't come through, and I will end up feeling foolish and alone.
11. I will fail doing it or look dumb.
12. If I am not successful or unable to complete the task, I fear people will think that I was insincere, not persistent, or inconsistent. I have a bigger fear of people incorrectly perceiving my motives.
13. If God hasn't already used me to bring my family to him, why should I expect other greater things to happen through me? Also, maybe I'm not old enough.
14. I think satisfaction with good keeps me from aiming at great. Sometimes I'm tempted to think, "What I'm doing makes a difference and that's good enough."
15. What I attempt will fail, I'll look dumb, and God will be seen as weak because of my failure.

Be encouraged. People who are "professionals" at ministry are struggling with the same lies you are. We must counter these lies with truth.

GOD'S TRUTH FOR YOU

God wants you to dream bigger than you have been. He wants you to ask him for even more than you can ask or imagine. Such requests honor him. He wants you to believe that "You Can" (through his power, of course). Whether your next step in ministry is to share your faith, start discipling someone, plant a church, or go to the unreached, you have all the power and resources of the Godhead available to you. Could training help you do it better? Probably, but don't let your lack of training keep you from action. Remember, those who have just a little training but take action make a much greater impact than well-trained people who take little action. We not only need to believe this for ourselves, but we also need to empower others with this truth. I believe that more harm has come to the advancement of the gospel from people saying, "You can't" than has come from people encouraging others to act who weren't quite ready.

God loves to use the young and ill-equipped to do great things for his glory. Think about David facing Goliath. Saul told David, "...You are not able to go against this Philistine to fight with him, for you are but a youth, and he has been a man of war from his youth" (1 Samuel 17:33 NIV). Aren't you glad David didn't listen to Saul when he told him he was too young and inexperienced?

The question is not, "Do you have enough power or resources to get the job done?" It is, "Will you believe the promises of Christ?" He is looking for people who will trust him. "For the eyes of the Lord range throughout the earth to strengthen those whose hearts are fully committed to him" (2 Chronicles 16:9). All of the resources of God are available to you in Christ. Unfortunately, most Christians are like Jed Clampett of the Beverly Hillbillies sitcom whose property was rich with oil, and he didn't even know it. He lived most of his life totally oblivious of the riches that he already possessed. He was a millionaire, but he didn't live like it because he was unaware of it. And the truth is that people don't usually act in ways that are inconsistent with the way they perceive themselves. The following story illustrates this well:

> An American Indian tells about a brave who found an eagle's egg and put it into a nest of a prairie chicken. The eaglet hatched with the brood of chicks and grew up with them.
>
> All his life, the changeling eagle, thinking he was a prairie chicken, did what the prairie chickens did. He scratched in the dirt for seeds

and insects to eat. He clucked and cackled. And he flew in a brief thrashing of wings and flurry of feathers no more than a few feet off the ground. After all, that's how prairie chickens were supposed to fly.

Years passed. And the changeling eagle grew very old. One day, he saw a magnificent bird far above him in the cloudless sky. Hanging with graceful majesty on the powerful wind currents, it soared with scarcely a beat of its strong golden wings.

"What a beautiful bird!" said the changeling eagle to his neighbor. "What is it?"

"That's an eagle—the chief of the birds," the neighbor clucked. "But don't give it a second thought. You could never be like him."

So the changeling eagle never gave it another thought. And it died thinking it was a prairie chicken.[107]

What were the eagle's chances of changing his behavior if his beliefs didn't change first? Not good. Believing the truth is key to your empowerment and that of your disciples'. Consider these promises that Christ, the great empowerer, has made to you:

- And Jesus answered them, "Truly, I say to you, if you have faith and do not doubt, you will not only do what has been done to the fig tree, but even *if you say to this mountain, 'Be taken up and thrown into the sea,' it will happen.*" (Matthew 21:21)
- "Truly, truly, I say to you, whoever believes in me *will also do the works that I do; and greater works than these* will he do, because I am going to the Father." (John 14:12)
- "Behold, *I have given you authority to tread on serpents and scorpions, and over all the power of the enemy*, and nothing shall hurt you." (Luke 10:19)
- "And behold, *I am with you always*, to the end of the age." (Matthew 28:20)

Adoniram Judson was right when he said, "The future is as bright as the promises of God!"

CLOSING EXERCISE:

If you knew for sure that God's power was upon you and that anything you attempted for him would succeed, what do you believe he would want you to attempt?

Would you be brave enough to write down that dream in the space below?

____

____

____

____

____

____

CHAPTER 11

FROM VISION TO REALITY

In the late 1990s, our family moved from Bangkok to northeast Thailand to start a campus ministry and church planting effort among an unreached group called the Isan people. Those were some sweet times as our team prayed and dreamed together about what God might do through us in our city and throughout the whole region. It has always been exciting to me to see a new ministry launched and then watch it become a full blown reality.

Not long after we moved to our new location, one of my Thai teammates, Dang, and I went to buy chairs for the church that didn't exist yet. I remember measuring off the top floor of the shop we had rented to see how many chairs would fit inside. When we were done, Dang and I stopped and begged God in prayer to multiply our lives and the lives of our teammates. We wanted to see those sixty new green chairs filled with former Buddhists who had fallen in love with Jesus.

When I think back at the joy of seeing that room filled and of how our vision became a reality, I recall Proverbs 13:19: "A desire fulfilled is sweet to the soul..." We have a gladness in Christ that is not dependent on our success in ministry, but at the same time there is a special delight that comes from seeing people enter the kingdom. "For what is our hope or joy or crown of boasting before our Lord Jesus at his coming? Is it not you?" (1 Thessalonians 2:19).

Unfortunately, even the best trained laborers don't often see their visions fulfilled. Their hopes of multiplying disciples for the glory of God never materialize. That is disappointing on many levels. As Proverbs 13:12 says, "Hope deferred makes the heart sick, but a desire fulfilled is a tree of life." The encouraging news is that it is possible for you to not only be a faithful disciple, but to be a *fruitful* disciple-maker, no matter the circumstances.

We have seen the importance of placing ourselves on teams and in movements that will assist and fuel our disciple-making efforts. We have looked at important behaviors and practices for multiplication. However, there are many people who function in disciple-making movements and have all the advantages that come from their context and training, yet fail to multiply. How can this be? There are clearly a few personal issues that factor in when it comes to successful multiplication. Immersion into a favorable context is no guarantee of personal fruitfulness. The Bible gives us at least four indispensable prerequisites for our visions to become realities.

PREREQUISITE ONE: DEVOTIONAL CONSISTENCY

A survey of 700 small group leaders revealed that leaders who spent ninety minutes or more in daily devotions multiplied their groups twice as much as those who spent less than half an hour. As time with the Lord increased, so did the leader's capacity to multiply his or her cell.[108] Should this surprise us in light of what Jesus said?

> Abide in me, and I in you. As the branch cannot bear fruit by itself, unless it abides in the vine, neither can you, unless you abide in me. I am the vine; you are the branches. Whoever abides in me and I in him, he it is that bears much fruit, for apart from me you can do nothing. (John 15:4-5)

Of course, abiding in Christ involves more than just spending time alone with God. It must be accompanied by living out in public what he shows us in private. But from where does the faith and encouragement to do that come? From frequently pulling away and allowing God to refill our tanks. Highly effective disciple-makers have learned that multiplication is a result of overflow, not overwork. You can never do enough for people if you are always with people. Jesus himself was constantly pulling away from ministry to be alone with the Father. We see the wisdom of this in the words of J. Hudson Taylor:

> Do not have your concert first, and then tune your instrument afterwards. Begin the day with the Word of God and prayer, and get first of all into harmony with Him.[109]

Want to bear fruit consistently? Plant yourself regularly in God's Word. Stay there until your faith is full and your heart is glad in his presence. Then you will have something to offer the world and will bear fruit consistently. As the psalmist says:

> But his delight is in the law of the Lord, and on his law he meditates day and night. He is like a tree planted by streams of water that yields its fruit in its season, and its leaf does not wither. In all that he does, he prospers. (Psalm 1:2-3)

Before moving on to the next prerequisite, stop and ask yourself, "Are my roots deep enough in the divine life that I am able to make disciples out of an overflow of my walk with God?" If not, run to him now. Fullness of joy and times of refreshment are awaiting you in his presence.[110]

PREREQUISITE TWO: DEATH TO OTHER VISIONS

You can't just tack disciple-making on to everything else you are doing and expect to succeed. It must be central. Your life must revolve around it. Without question, lifelong spiritual multiplication will require your vision to be singular. In the context of talking with his disciples about their vision and the potential for them to have an eternal impact, Jesus warned his disciples that having two visions would create such a conflict that they would certainly fail at one of them.

> No one can serve two masters, for either he will hate the one and love the other, or he will be devoted to the one and despise the other. You cannot serve God and money. (Matthew 6:24)

The fact is that you only have so many hours in a day. Many of those hours are taken up with the necessities of life, and we are left with only a small amount of discretionary time. How you spend that time will be determined by what it is you really value. If your heart is set on being rich, you will spend those hours seeking money. If your passion is for the pleasures of this world, they will be your pursuit. If you're not careful to set your vision squarely on eternal impact, other things will come in and choke your disciple-making efforts. Jesus spoke plainly about these enemies of multiplication. Remember that wonderful promise of a multiplying life in Mark?

> But those that were sown on the good soil are the ones who hear the word and accept it and bear fruit, thirtyfold and sixtyfold and a hundredfold. (Mark 4:20)

Right before this promise, Jesus mentioned three enemies of multiplication:

1. The cares of this world
2. The deceitfulness of riches
3. The desires for other things

> And others are the ones sown among thorns. They are those who hear the word, but the cares of the world and the deceitfulness of riches and the desires for other things enter in and choke the word, and it proves unfruitful. (Mark 4:18-19)

For your vision of multiplication to become a reality, you must die to all distractions that other visions and desires create. The apostle Paul made the need for single-minded focus clear to Timothy right after telling him to reproduce in "faithful men":

> No soldier gets entangled in civilian pursuits, since his aim is to please the one who enlisted him. (2 Timothy 2:4)

IDENTIFYING COMPETING VISIONS

What makes the dangers mentioned by Jesus particularly hazardous is that they slowly creep into our hearts without declaring their presence. Enemies we are aware of can be avoided. For example, rattlesnakes are extremely poisonous, but very few people die from them because they usually announce their presence. Lightning, on the other hand, is more dangerous because you don't know when it is about to strike. In fact, in the United States, you are nine times more likely to die from lightning than from any venomous snake.[111] Silent enemies are by far the most dangerous ones we face.

Rarely do people admit to me that the reason they aren't multiplying their life is because they are too concerned about earning extra money. When we think about materialistic people, we never think about ourselves.

Since recognizing our enemies is the first step to defeating them, would you take just a minute now to prayerfully reflect on your own heart and life and answer the following:

1. What is the biggest care of this world that jeopardizes my spiritual multiplication?

   ____

   ____

2. What is the main way the deceitfulness of riches is limiting my impact on eternity?

   ____

   ____

3. What are the top two other things that I desire which are most negatively thwarting my personal ministry?

   ____

   ____

In his book *Radical*, David Platt points out the time in American history when the majority of the church was deceived into thinking that the form of slavery practiced in the United States was somehow okay.[112] He raises the question of whether or not we could currently be corporately deceived in the area of materialism. Are the things we consider normal and basic life necessities not what God intends for us? Could they actually be keeping us from experiencing life at its fullest?

Undoubtedly, we need to reevaluate how we spend our money, but what about how we spend our time? I'm wondering if the same could be true with our view of sports or television or hobbies. I enjoy playing and watching sports, and I don't think it is sin to do so. However, just like eating can become gluttony when done in excess, so recreation can become a waste of one's life when overdone. My concern is that what we now consider normal and even needed is so widely accepted in our culture. No one questions a lifestyle so consumed with recreation that no time is left for ministry. Our kids have to play every sport in season, or we will not be doing our job as parents, right? Some of my Muslim friends don't see it that way.

Their kids play sports, too, but not so much that they don't have significant time to memorize the Qur'an when they come home from school. Are we modeling the value of time in God's Word for our kids and disciples, or are we showing them how to waste their free time? Remember, I enjoy sports too, but I can't help but question the huge amounts of time we spend watching and playing them when we could be investing our lives in eternal things—people. The words of the great missionary statesman C.T. Studd come to mind:

Some men die by shrapnel.
Some men die by flames.
Most men die inch by inch,
playing silly little games.[113]

We are definitely passing along our values to our children. The question is not *if* you are passing something along, it is *what* are you passing on. Here is a sobering passage:

> They would not listen, however, but persisted in their former practices. Even while these people were worshiping the Lord, they were serving their idols. To this day their children and grandchildren continue to do as their ancestors did. (2 Kings 17:40-41)

Whether you have physical children or not, you are hopefully reproducing spiritually, or at least desiring to do so, and that makes dealing with your idols crucial. All the ministry principles I shared will be of no use to you if you don't smash your idols. These are the enemies of multiplication mentioned by Jesus. The good news is that if you die to these parasites, multiplication follows.

> Very truly I tell you, unless a kernel of wheat falls to the ground and dies, it remains only a single seed. But if it dies, it produces many seeds. (John 12:24)

A divided heart with competing visions is not the only threat to multiplication. In marriage, because two people become one, anything less than total alignment on the same vision of multiplication will greatly diminish one's impact.

MARRIAGE AND VISION

I have seen many aspiring disciple-makers marry people who don't really value disciple-making. Instead of being partners together in fulfilling the Great Commission, they end up in constant tension with each other about how to spend their time and money. This divided vision lessens the impact of the one who really wanted to make disciples.

Singles, please choose well, realizing that being equally yoked means marrying someone who shares your purpose in life—loving Jesus *and* multiplying disciples. What's the best way to know if they do? Look at how they spent their time last year. What I said about selecting disciples holds true for selecting a mate too: "Selection without observation is presumption." Don't marry someone who can articulate a great vision. Marry someone who has lived one.

What if you are already married and your spouse doesn't share your vision of multiplying disciples? First, love and honor your mate with all of your strength. Second, as you will probably have less time and energy to invest in people, realize that a multiplying approach to ministry is even more important for *you* than it is for someone who is married to another disciple-maker. Make sure to invest your limited resources well in people who will reproduce your impact. All hope is not lost. Remember the story in Chapter Two of how God multiplied the small and feeble efforts of David and Svea Flood through one small boy? Boldly ask God to do the same with your life! However, your vision will never become a reality until you develop a plan to turn your intentions into action.

PREREQUISITE THREE: DEVELOPMENT OF A PLAN

> The plans of the diligent lead surely to abundance,
> but everyone who is hasty comes only to poverty.
> (Proverbs 21:5)

There are a few essentials of any good spiritual multiplication plan. Let's look at those first.

1. WRITE OUT YOUR VISION AND PLAN.

It's good to have the vision in your head and heart, but putting it on paper will help you refine it and motivate others with it.

> And the Lord answered me: "Write the vision; make it plain on tablets, so he may run who reads it." (Habakkuk 2:2)

2. GET SPECIFIC ABOUT WHAT YOU ARE TRUSTING GOD TO DO.

I believe that the more specific we are, the more glory God gets when vision becomes reality. Ask God to give you specific goals with which to trust him. Be sure to have specific promises from God's Word that you are praying and asking him to keep.

3. SHARE YOUR VISION AND PLAN WITH OTHERS, ASKING THEM TO JOIN YOU.

Personal goals and New Year's resolutions often fail because they aren't shared. Several years ago, I heard about a movie called *The Bucket List,* starring Jack Nicholson and Morgan Freeman. After that, I saw a slew of websites created that encouraged people to make their own bucket list. I was never impressed with the concept until I actually watched the movie and learned that the two main characters didn't each make their own list, but made a list together. That's genius! How about getting together with a few close friends and making a corporate bucket list of what you would like to see God do through your lives?

4. PIN YOUR PLAN UP IN A VISIBLE PLACE.

We are prone to get off-track and can therefore benefit from frequent reminders of our purpose and goals. Take a few key parts of those goals (like your bucket list) and make them your screen saver or tape them inside your Bible.

The following is a very simple starter template for your plan. (If you have a spouse or close friend who shares your vision, be sure to write your plan together.)

MY DISCIPLE-MAKING PLAN

Vision – I would like to see the following vision become a reality:

Trusting God – I am trusting God to do the following:

Before I die:

In the next three years:

In the next twelve months:

In the next three months:

I am claiming the following promises from God's Word:

Sharing the vision – I will ask the following people to join me in the vision and to speak into it:

Pin it up – I will put a visual reminder in the following places:

POSSIBLE ACTIONS TO INCLUDE IN YOUR PLAN

Your personal circumstances will determine the direction you should take with your plan. Below are a few possible actions for you to consider. Check all that seem to describe an appropriate action for you to include in your plan.

- ❏ I am in a church or ministry that functions as a disciple-making movement. I will talk with my leadership about what next steps I should take to see my vision become a reality.
- ❏ I will seek out and join a church or ministry that functions as a disciple-making team.
- ❏ I will challenge some young believers to join a disciple-making team (DMT) I will lead. (Consider using *Foundations: Missional Community Guidebook* to help you lead this group.)
- ❏ I will challenge some existing leaders to join a "Turbo Team" I will lead to expose them to this material and model for them how to function as a DMT. The goal of a Turbo Team is to help existing small group leaders learn as quickly as possible how to become disciple-making team leaders. (Consider using *Spiritual Multiplication in the Real World: Missional Community Study Guide* to help you lead this group.)
- ❏ I have a desire to make disciples among the unreached. I will seek out an opportunity to learn cross-cultural disciple-making. (Consider writing us at goer@spiritualmultiplication.org for help.)
- ❏ I feel that God has given me a heart for missions and the gift of leadership. I will seek out ways to develop myself as a leader. (Consider contacting missionleader@spiritualmultiplication.org to learn about how we can help disciple and mentor you to lead a team going to the unreached, or help a team of mobilizers who disciple and send others to the unreached.)
- ❏ I am a church or ministry leader and would like help training my staff in disciple-making. I will seek out some help. (Consider writing us at leader@spiritualmultiplication.org to find out how we or those we know can help.)

REALITY CHECK

It would be great if everyone reading this book was a member of a church that functions as a disciple-making movement or could easily join one. In reality, though, most readers will need to be a part of a disciple-making team that functions apart from a movement. Don't despair. There is good news. It is possible for individual teams to succeed! Small bands of like-minded believers can provide all of the essential elements that aspiring disciple-makers need. It doesn't matter whether they are a house church or a disciple-making team functioning under a larger church that doesn't necessarily function as a movement. We've seen them thrive and multiply! For that to happen, though, these teams require the three crucial elements covered in the next section. You would do well to make sure your plan ensures all three of these.

ESSENTIAL ELEMENTS FOR TEAMS TO SUCCEED OUTSIDE OF A DISCIPLE-MAKING MOVEMENT

1. A UNITY OF PURPOSE—EVANGELISM AND MULTIPLICATION

All of the successful groups we observed came together primarily for the purpose of helping each other evangelize and multiply. None of the groups made the growth of the members in the group their primary objective, yet you can find consistent testimonials of tremendous growth in all the groups. No one transitioned an existing growth-oriented group into an evangelistic team, and we would not recommend you try it. Members can come from other groups, but the safest way to ensure that all of the members are on board with the vision is to start a new team. No one is in the group unless they intentionally decide to join! They must understand that it is a different type of group than they have been a part of in the past.

At times, it may be hard to tell the difference between a typical small group of Christians and a disciple-making team. Both meet regularly, pray, study the Word, fellowship, and maybe even talk about evangelism. But there is something that a disciple-making team has that standard small groups don't—evangelism is their primary purpose, and they do it together.

Ceiling fans and helicopters are similar in many ways. Both have motors, blades that spin, and people sitting under them. Though they look somewhat alike, there is a reason why your ceiling fan doesn't fly away.

That's not its purpose. A ceiling fan is designed to make you comfortable (like many small groups), and a helicopter is designed to take you somewhere (like a disciple-making team). Helicopter blades are not like giant ceiling fan blades that just push air down. If they were, helicopters would never get off the ground. They are actually like small airplane wings that spin and create lift. I don't know about you, but I need the lift others can give me when it comes to evangelism. Make sure the group you are in doesn't just look similar to an evangelistic team; it should actually function as one.

Isn't it ironic that we come together for Bible study and prayer but then send each other out to do evangelism by ourselves? Unfortunately, if we do ministry together, it is usually only meeting physical needs and doesn't address evangelism. When we *do* team up to do evangelism, it is often just for short-term mission trips. After these trips, we all admit that the week doing evangelism together was the most fruitful and personally challenging week of the year. Yet what do we do after that week? We spend the next fifty-one weeks trying to do evangelism by ourselves. Why do we do this?

Most believers would be capable of helping someone *grow* in Christ if they ever *led* someone to Christ. The logjam in the spiritual multiplication process is that most of us don't lead people to Christ on a regular basis. Teaming up with other disciple-makers to focus on evangelism will help you remedy this.

2. LEADERSHIP

Each of the disciple-making teams we studied had one or more leaders who kept the group focused on their purpose and led them week-by-week in simple activities to accomplish it. Nothing they did required super management skills, but their leadership was crucial to turn a group of Christians into a team of laborers. To help you do this, we put together the guidebooks mentioned earlier. Whether you use these guidebooks or not, you will constantly need to fight the natural tendency of Christian groups to move away from outreach and toward an inward focus.

Leading a disciple-making team is different than leading a Bible study. You don't have to know a lot to be qualified to do it. You do, however, have to be willing to set the example in making time with lost friends a priority. Don't count yourself out if you are currently struggling to do so. The team will help you do it! You may remember I shared about struggling to get consistent time with the lost a couple of years ago. I started a new disciple-making team that helped me with this. It has now been about a year and a half since our team started, and we have already seen over twenty people come to Christ! Though I started the team, a guy I'm discipling leads it now. In a few months, we will multiply into two or three teams. I won't be leading any of the teams because other leaders have been raised up. But you can bet I'll still be on one of the teams because I continue to need the accountability, encouragement, and teamwork they provide.

3. A CHURCH WHO WANTS TO SEE IT HAPPEN

Each time we saw a disciple-making team succeed, the mother church or churches were not opposed to the formation of the team. The fact that a church doesn't perfectly function as a disciple-making movement need not be an obstacle to a disciple-making team forming and multiplying if the pastors and elders are supportive. If, however, the church leadership is not on board, we would not recommend for you to press ahead. You need to bless and support your leaders. If you can't do that for one reason or another, you should move on to another church rather than becoming a distraction and burden to the leaders and the ministry of your present church. This is a last resort. By all means, try to make it work within your existing church first as long as you have the blessing of your leaders.

So far we have seen that the following are prerequisites to your vision becoming a reality:

- Devotional life consistency
- Death to other visions
- Development of a plan

While these are critical, no significant disciple-making ministry has ever come into existence without God-inspired determination and perseverance.

PREREQUISITE FOUR: DETERMINATION

You will experience times of discouragement and defeat as you pursue your vision. The question is not whether or not these times will come, but how you will respond. Will you hold up or fold up? You must press through them with determination if you ever want to see your vision become a reality. I am not speaking about sucking it up in your own strength, pulling yourself up by your bootstraps, and gutting it out like the world tells you to. I am talking about relying on God's strength to persevere. God-enabled determination is needed. Two verses will direct you:

> And let us not grow weary of doing good, for in due season we will reap, if we do not give up. (Galatians 6:9)

> Therefore, my beloved brothers, be steadfast, immovable, always abounding in the work of the Lord, knowing that in the Lord your labor is not in vain. (1 Corinthians 15:58)

Times of discouragement and defeat will come from both personal sin and ministry failure. We must be ready.

DISCOURAGEMENT FROM PERSONAL SIN

Hopefully, you are a person who has a tender heart and is sensitive to the Holy Spirit's conviction of sin. A conscience that is pricked by even "little sins" is a good thing. The danger is that we will not just listen to the Holy Spirit, but also to the accuser of the saints. Satan will condemn us and tell us that we are too sinful to make disciples.

Paul knew that if Timothy was going to persevere in disciple-making, he must learn to find strength in God's grace. This reliance certainly included finding hope when experiencing discouragement because of personal sin. Before he laid on Timothy the challenge to reproduce spiritually (2 Timothy 2:2), he first told him of an indispensable prerequisite to multiplying—"You then, my son, *be strong in the grace* that is in Christ Jesus" (2 Timothy 2:1 NIV). God's grace is inexhaustible. If you think you have somehow used it up, you are dead wrong. Remember what Jesus told Peter to do after he sinned by denying him three times: "And when you have turned again, strengthen your brothers" (Luke 22:32).

The beauty of doing ministry together as a team is that you don't have to fight sin alone. Some sins can knock us down again and again and again.

When we find ourselves in a losing battle, it is crucial to have a band of believers to help pick us up. As Solomon says,

> Two are better than one, because they have a good reward for their toil. For if they fall, one will lift up his fellow. But woe to him who is alone when he falls and has not another to lift him up! (Ecclesiastes 4:9-10)

When I read these verses, I remember being a pledge in my fraternity. One night, our brothers blindfolded all the new pledges and marched us out into the woods. We clung to each other as we walked deeper and deeper into the forest. It would have been hard enough to walk at night in the woods without a flashlight, but the blindfolds made us completely blind. As we tripped and stumbled over roots and fallen branches, we held fast to each other and picked each other up when we fell.

Things got even harder for us when we were led into what seemed like the world's biggest and thickest mud puddle. We stood shoulder to shoulder with our arms locked, standing up to our knees in an unforgiving mixture of mud and near-freezing water. Our instructions were to hit the deck when we heard the sound of enemy fighter planes flying over and shooting at us (sound effects provided by the brothers) and then to stand back up when they were gone. It didn't take long for us to learn that we needed each other if we were going to survive this object lesson. Pity the man who fell and didn't have a brother close by to lift him up.

FEELINGS OF DEFEAT FROM FAILED ATTEMPTS TO MULTIPLY

Failed attempts to multiply are not really the problem. But not expecting them or misinterpreting them can be deadly. If you don't expect to fail and then you do, what state of mind will you be in? What impact will that have on your perseverance? We must expect to ultimately succeed but to fail often along the way. Trust God that your failures will not be fatal. They are learning opportunities along the path to your vision becoming a reality.

When I first attempted to disciple others, I challenged four young men into a discipleship group. It went from four to one in just a few months. I made lots of rookie mistakes. Since that time I have never made another mistake. Just kidding. Clearly, I have had some wins and some losses over the last three decades of disciple-making. The amazing thing, though, is that somehow, in spite of all of my sin and mistakes, God has been faithful to keep his end of the bargain and multiply my feeble attempts.

I love what Michael Jordan says about his career:

> I've missed more than 9,000 shots in my career. I've lost almost 300 games. Twenty-six times, I've been trusted to take the game winning shot and missed. I've failed over and over and over again in my life. And that is why I succeed.[114]

Those who succeed in life are not usually those who are the most gifted, but those who are the most persistent. As author Napoleon Hill observed:

> I had the happy privilege of analyzing both Mr. Edison and Mr. Ford, year by year, over a long period of years, and therefore, the opportunity to study them at close range, so I speak from actual knowledge when I say that I found no quality save PERSISTENCE, in either of them, that even remotely suggested the major source of their stupendous achievements.[115]

A ministry of exponentially multiplying disciples comes as a result of determined persistence in the right direction over the long haul. The process will be long, arduous, and full of setbacks. If you keep at it and learn as you go, your labor will not be in vain. Don't give up!

The writer of the book of Hebrews was concerned about the perseverance of his readers. One of the dangers he knew they faced was the possibility of misinterpreting the difficulties they were experiencing. In chapter twelve, he stresses that they should not interpret hardship as God being against them, or not having his hand on them. He wants them to see hardship as discipline from a loving father. This discipline he points out is actually proof that God has not abandoned them or forsaken them. Properly interpreted, hardship is a reason for encouragement and perseverance. Please don't let failures and difficulties defeat you. Don't quit. Rather, understand that God is using them to beautify you for the glory of his son, your bridegroom. If you fail and fall, continue to depend on God. He will help you get back up and keep going. Your father is cheering you on!

NOW WHAT?

I want to leave you with a statement of your mission that is not an improvement on what Jesus told his disciples, but simply an explanation of what they understood him to mean by it. So here it is…

As part of a disciple-making team,
go and multiply *disciple-making teams* in all nations.

We must stop trying to minister as individuals and start functioning as disciple-making teams. Our goal must change too. Instead of going out and attempting to multiply individual disciples, we must set our sights on multiplying disciple-making communities. The Great Commission tells us to baptize new believers into "the name of the Father and of the Son and of the Holy Spirit" (Matthew 28:19). The Godhead lives in glorious community and functions as a redemptive team. As we abide in him and live and minister in community with each other, he will be with us always. He enables us to multiply his children in all nations. As our vision of spiritual multiplication in the real world becomes a reality, we will see worshippers become as numerous as the stars in the sky and the sand on the seashore. His glory will cover the earth as the waters cover the sea.

Can you believe he lets us be a part of this?!

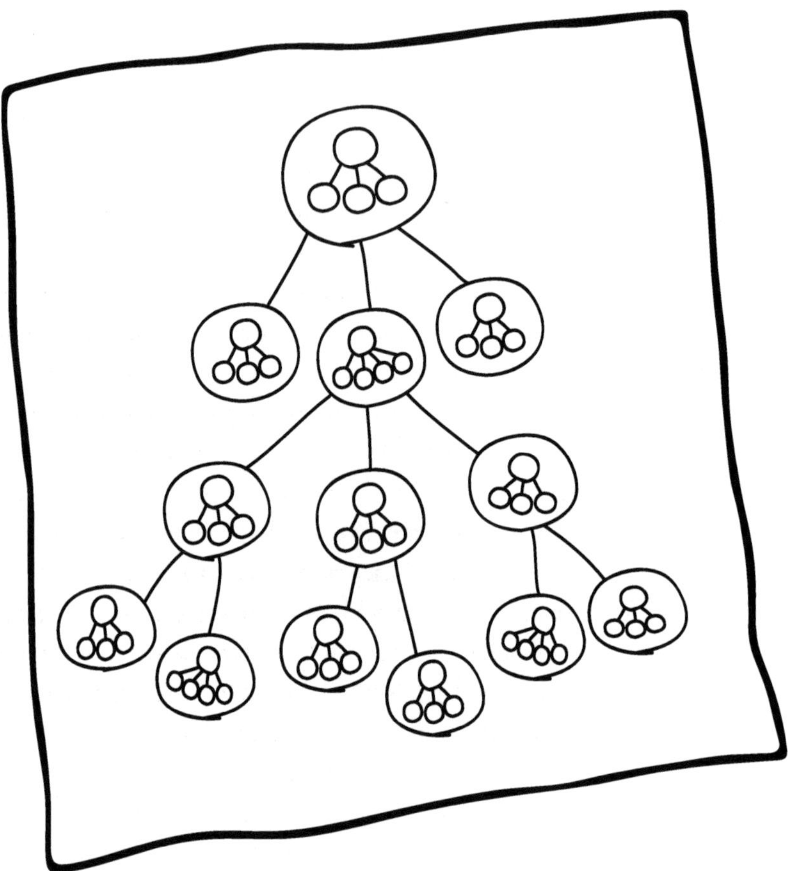

Could it be time to start using a new multiplication diagram? Maybe one like this?

APPENDIX 1

NOTE TO PASTORS

I have watched several pastors struggle with trying to meet all the demands of preaching weekly, leading staff and business meetings, pastoral care, etc., plus discipling and equipping others in a life-on-life way. These pastors have wanted to break free of all of the demands and opportunities of the macro ministry to invest deeply in the micro (personal disciple-making) but somehow never have succeeded in doing so. I thank the Lord for other men whom I have watched deeply invest in the lives of others even though they led megachurches. How did they do it? At the end of the day, there is only one answer to that question: correct priorities. Those who succeeded viewed their ministry first and foremost as one of equipping others to multiply their lives through life-on-life missional discipleship, and they prioritized their lives accordingly. They had to decide that, as much as they loved to preach, they wouldn't do it every week, and that they would turn down a lot of other great opportunities and "open doors." We see this in the life of the apostle Paul. He turned down a tremendous "open door" to preach the gospel to thousands of college students alongside John Piper. (Just checking to see if you're awake.) Seriously though, look what he did when faced with the choice between taking a great preaching opportunity and going to find *one* of the men in whom he was investing:

> When I came to Troas to preach the gospel of Christ, even though a door was opened for me in the Lord, my spirit was not at rest because I did not find my brother Titus there. So I took leave of them and went on to Macedonia. (2 Corinthians 2:12-13)

Pastor, do you have a few key people into whom you are actively pouring your life? Are they close enough to you to see how you live and minister? Do they see you sharing your faith on a regular basis? Are you making the tough choices needed to multiply *laborers* and not just fill pew seats?

APPENDIX 2

QUESTIONS TO AID IN MEDITATION

- How can I apply this?
- Why haven't I applied this better in the past?
- If I were to apply this, what changes would it require in my attitude? Behavior?
- What aspect of God's character requires that I apply this truth to my life?
- What would be the long-term and far-reaching effects of applying this truth to my life?
- What would they be if I didn't apply this truth to my life?
- Think of an example of when Jesus applied this truth (write it down).
- Who do I know that applies this truth consistently?
- What do I need to *trust God to do* regarding the application of this to my life?
- What is *my part* in applying this truth to my life?
- Visualize myself living out this truth in the different situations that come up in my daily life.

* Don't let the word "Visualize" scare you because it sounds New Age. There is nothing wrong with Christians imagining themselves applying God's righteous laws in the different circumstances of life they will encounter. This is a pleasing use of our God-given imagination. This practice will help you think through ahead of time how to respond in a godly way to those situations.

ENDNOTES

CHAPTER 1

[1] Some people attribute this quotation to Mark Twain.

[2] Psalm 127:3 and Proverbs 17:6

[3] 1 Thessalonians 2:19-20 and 3 John 1:4

[4] Genesis 12:7, 13:15, and 15:18

[5] Win Arn and Charles Arn, *The Master's Plan for Making Disciples: Every Christian an Effective Witness Through an Enabling Church* (Grand Rapids: Baker Books, 1998), 23.

[6] Michael J. Wilkins, *Following the Master* (Grand Rapids: Zondervan, 1992), 61-63.

CHAPTER 2

[7] Aggie Hurst, *One Witness* (New Jersey: Fleming H. Revell Company, 1986).

[8] Ibid., 13.

[9] Ibid., 14.

CHAPTER 3

[10] Dwight D. Eisenhower, *Crusade in Europe* (Baltimore: The Johns Hopkins University Press, 1997), 36.

[11] For the complete survey instrument, go to www.spiritualmultiplication.org.

CHAPTER 4

[12] When I speak of disciple-making movements in this book, I am referring to ministries or churches that are made up of multiple disciple-making teams. These teams benefit from their association together and receive some level of coaching and centralized leadership. Recently, a number of speakers and authors have begun to use the phrase disciple-making movement in place of church planting movement. They have made this change because they feel it better captures their goal.

[13] Mark 8:35

[14] 1 Timothy 3 and Titus 1

[15] Some have said that the New Testament church started on the day of Pentecost. I believe this is wrong for the following reasons:

1. There was already a group of followers of Jesus.
2. There were leaders for the group.
3. The group met together.
4. The group had a common purpose.
5. There was already a practice of administering the Sacraments.

CHAPTER 5

[16] A seeker service is a style of worship and teaching that is geared toward lost individuals who are investigating Christianity rather than equipping the saints.

[17] Joel Comiskey, *Home Cell Group Explosion* (Houston: Touch Publications, 2000), 29–32.

[18] David Garrison, *Church Planting Movements* (Richmond: International Mission Board of the Southern Baptist Convention, 1999), 4.

[19] My usage of the word organic is not in response to Neil Cole's helpful book on the subject of church multiplication.

[20] Dave Ferguson and Jon Ferguson, *Exponential: How You and Your Friends Can Start a Missional Church Movement* (Grand Rapids: Zondervan, 2010), 118.

[21] Ibid., 95.

[22] David Garrison, *Church Planting Movements: How God Is Redeeming a Lost World* (Midlothian: WIGTake Resources, 2004), 172.

[23] Matthew 11:7, 13:2, 14:14, 15:30, and 19:2

CHAPTER 6

[24] I believe that having a good marriage has as much to do with your behavior after marriage as it does with your selection of "the right mate." However, mate selection does matter.

[25] Matthew 13:44-45, Luke 9:23-25, and Mark 10:29-30

[26] 2 Corinthians 5:9

[27] In suggesting that we expose non-believers to loving Christian community, I am not recommending "extraction evangelism." In fact, in most cases, it is best to encourage seekers and new believers to immediately share what they are observing and learning with their family and friends (Mark 5:18-20 and John 4:39).

[28] I've shared with you several of the tools that we saw God use in creating interest. There are others—like dreams or conversations about man's depravity and hell—that we haven't discussed.

[29] Matthew 5:21-48

[30] Galatians 3:24

[31] The Bridge Diagram, the Four Spiritual Laws, the Evangelism Explosion presentation, or some other tool that you have contextualized can all be used along with books, MP3s, the Jesus film, and evangelistic retreats and Bible studies. If someone is interested, almost any tool will be helpful. If they are not, nothing will work.

[32] I am aware that some who are involved in Muslim evangelism may disagree with the idea of bringing new believers into close kingdom community. But I believe that team evangelism and exposing non-believers to kingdom community are biblical princi-

ples and therefore should not be abandoned when evangelizing in a Muslim context with the vision of starting a church planting movement. To do so could keep a movement from ever starting or from growing in a healthy way. A contextualized application of the principle of team evangelism is to just keep the teams very small.

CHAPTER 7

[33] Steve Shadrach, *The Fuel and the Flame* (Atlanta: Authentic, 2003), 148.

[34] Allen Hadidian, *Discipleship: Helping Other Christians to Grow* (Chicago: Moody Press, 1987), 45.

[35] Mark 3:14

[36] Ephesians 1:15-23 and 3:14-19; Romans 1:10 and 10:1; 2 Corinthians 13:7, 9; Ephesians 1:16-17 and 3:16; Philippians 1:4, 9-11; Colossians 1:3-4, 9-12; 1 Thessalonians 1:2 and 3:10; 2 Thessalonians 1:11-12; 2 Timothy 1:3; and Philemon 1:4-6

[37] Joel Comiskey, *Cell-Based Ministry as a Positive Factor for Church Growth in Latin America* (Ph.D. diss., Fuller Theological Seminary School of World Mission, 1997), 261.

[38] Gary L. Thomas, *Sacred Pathways: Discover Your Soul's Path to God* (Grand Rapids: Zondervan, 2000).

[39] David Garrison, *Church Planting Movements* (Richmond: International Mission Board of the Southern Baptist Convention, 1999), 16.

[40] *The Personal Growth Series*, The Navigators. Used by permission of NavPress, Colorado Springs, CO (www.navpress.com). All rights reserved.

[41] 1 Corinthians 8:1

[42] Ephesians 1:15-23; 3:14-19; 6:13; 1 Corinthians 3:11; 15:3-6; and 1 Peter 5:9

[43] Proverbs 11:14 and 15:22

[44] Acts 13:50

[45] Acts 14:6

[46] Acts 14:19

[47] For a list of resources that may be helpful in this area, please check www.spiritualmultiplication.org.

CHAPTER 8

[48] John 17:17, 1 Thessalonians 5:23, and Hebrews 12:10

[49] Philippians 1:6 and Romans 8:29

[50] 2 Corinthians 3:18

[51] A.W. Tozer, *The Knowledge of the Holy* (New York: Harper Collins, 1961), 1.

[52] Matthew 7:5 (Obviously, we must be humble and introspective in the process!)

[53] Romans 12:2

[54] Neil Anderson, *Steps to Freedom in Christ: The Step by Step Guide to Freedom in Christ* (USA: Gospel Light, 2001).

[55] A harmony of the gospels is a book that lays out parallel passages from the gospels and makes it easier to understand the chronology of Jesus' ministry among other things.

[56] Luke 6:13

[57] Matthew 4:19 and Mark 1:17

[58] Robert E. Coleman, *The Master Plan of Evangelism*, (Grand Rapids: Fleming H. Revell Company, 1963), 24.

[59] Acts 1:21-22

[60] Mark 3:14

[61] Allen Hadidian, *Discipleship* (Moody Press: Chicago, 1979), 45.

[62] See www.spiritualmultiplication.org.

CHAPTER 9

[63] Keith Green's pamphlet "Why You Should Go to the Mission Field" may be found at www.lastdaysministries.org.

[64] The Barna Group Ltd, *Godless Hollywood? Bible Belt? New Research Exploring Faith in America's Largest Markets Produces Surprises.* Barna Group. Last modified 2009. http://www.barna.org/barna-update/article/5-barna-update/173-godless-hollywood-bible-belt-new-research-exploring-faith-in-americas-largest-markets-produces-surprises.

[65] "Shaikh of Bangladesh Ethnic People Profile." *Joshua Project*. Accessed March 13, 2013. http://www.joshuaproject.net/people-profile.php?peo3=18084&rog3=BG.

[66] Abram Huyser Honig, "Study Questions Whether Short-Term Missions Make a Difference," *Christianity Today*. Last modified 2005. http://www.christianitytoday.com/ct/2005/juneweb-only/12.0c.html.

[67] www.perspectives.org

[68] This is why I started teaching a four-hour long seminar called *Align*, which is designed to reveal God's global plan and challenge participants to align their lives with it. Visit www.spiritualmultiplication.org to find out how you can host an *Align* seminar. Other possibilities you should consider are:

- Taking or hosting a Perspectives course (www.perspectives.org)
- Leading a small group through a seven week study called *Xplore*, which explores God's Word, God's World, and God's Work (www.cmmpress.org)

[69] www.joshuaproject.net

[70] Romans 15:20

[71] Acts 20:24

[72] Revelation 7:9

[73] Kenneth Chan, "Interview: Dr. Ralph D. Winter, Founder of the United States Center for World Mission," *Christian Post*, 2005, accessed March 13, 2013, http://www.christianpost.com/news/interview-dr-ralph-d-winter-founder-of-the-united-states-center-for-world-mission-15542.

[74] See www.launchglobal.org for information about communities that are designed to help aspiring missionaries prepare to go.

[75] 2 Timothy 4:11

[76] www.joshuaproject.net

[77] Ralph D. Winter et al., "The Amazing Countdown Facts" accessed October 8, 2013, http://joshuaproject.net/assets/articles/amazing-countdown-facts.pdf.

[78] Deuteronomy 20:5-9

[79] Admittedly, researchers have had trouble locating the ad, and some have therefore questioned its existence. There seems to be no doubt, though, that Shackleton received an overwhelming number of applicants to accompany him on his journey. PBS, "Shackleton's Team." Nova Online, March 2002, accessed October 24, 2014, http://www.pbs.org/wgbh/nova/shackleton/1914/team.html.

[80] Shanda Oakley, "Not Home Yet," *A Pause on the Path*, January 30, 2012, http://www.shandaoakleyinspires.com/2012/01/not-home-yet.html.

CHAPTER 10

[81] John 8:32

[82] John 8:44

[83] Matthew 28:18

[84] John 14:14, Matthew 28:20, and 10:19

[85] John 14:12

[86] Ephesians 4:11-12

[87] Acts 9:27, 11:25, 14:12

[88] Some readers may think, "Well Saul had considerable Bible training before coming to Christ." It is true that he had a good base of knowledge, but up until his conversion, everything he had learned led him to believe that Christians were completely wrong and needed to be imprisoned or killed. Certainly someone with such strong opposing beliefs couldn't all of a sudden "get it" and be ready to become a witness for Christ, could he? Apparently he could.

[89] Douglas Hyde, *Dedication and Leadership* (Notre Dame: University of Notre Dame Press, 1966), 42-45.

[90] William Y. Smith, "Can Short-Term Teams Foster Long-Term Church-Planting Movements?" *Mission Frontiers*, January-February 2012, accessed March 13, 2013, http://www.missionfrontiers.org/issue/article/can-short-term-teams-foster-long-term-church-planting-movements.

[91] *Comiskey,* dissertation, p. 263.

[92] Neil Cole, *Organic Church: Growing Faith Where Life Happens* (San Francisco: Jossey-Bass, 2005), 149-150.

[93] William Y. Smith, "Can Short-Term Teams Foster Long-Term Church-Planting Movements?" Mission Frontiers, January-February 2012, accessed March 13, 2013, http://www.missionfrontiers.org/issue/article/can-short-term-teams-foster-long-term-church-planting-movements.

[94] The International Mission Board (IMB), which is the missionary sending arm of the Southern Baptist Convention, City Team, E3 Partners, United World Mission, and other prominent sending agencies are working diligently to crush Satan's lies about what it takes to plant a church. In the areas of the world where they have been successful at empowering people this way, the church is multiplying and expanding at staggering rates. See *Church Planting Movements* by David Garrison or *Miraculous Movements* by Jerry Trousdale.

[95] David Garrison, *Church Planting Movements: How God Is Redeeming a Lost World* (Midlothian: WIGTake Resources, 2004), 62.

[96] While I am encouraging us to affirm and validate these simple forms of church and therefore empower more people to plant and multiply churches, I want to put out a word of caution to house church members and advocates. House churches are not the only model of biblical church and are not necessarily superior to larger churches. Our research shows no correlation between church size and effectiveness in disciple-making. There are some giant churches out there that are knocking it out of the park when it comes to helping their members multiply, and there are churches that meet in homes that are equally effective. Let's validate both forms and empower people to plant and grow both.

[97] J.D. Payne, "Casting a Vision for Church Multiplication: 5 Steps to Consider," *Missiologically Thinking*, August 13, 2012, http://www.jdpayne.org/2012/08/13/casting-a-vision-for-church-multiplication-5-steps-to-consider.

[98] 1 Timothy 3:1-13 and Titus 1:5-9

[99] David Garrison, *Church Planting Movements: How God Is Redeeming a Lost World* (Midlothian: WIGTake Resources, 2004), 40, 89, 191.

[100] Soeren Kern, "Muslims Converting Empty European Churches into Mosques." *Gatestone Institute*, January 16, 2012, accessed March 13, 2013, http://www.gatestoneinstitute.org/2761/converting-churches-into-mosques.

[101] W. Wilson Cash, foreword to *Spontaneous Expansion of the Church,* by Roland Allen (London: World Dominion Press, 1949).

[102] Steve Murrell, *Youth on Fire: How God Uses Youth to Shake Nations and Shape History* (Pasig City: Every Nation Productions, 2001).

[103] Joel Comiskey, *Home Cell Group Explosion* (Houston: Touch Publications, 2000), 29-32.

[104] J.D. Payne, "Time to Enlarge the Church Planting Table," *Missiologically Thinking,* March 9, 2012, http://www.jdpayne.org/2012/03/09/time-to-enlarge-the-church-planting-table.

[105] Leslie T. Lyall, *A Passion for the Impossible: The Continuing Story of the Mission Hudson Taylor Began* (London: OMF Books, 1965), 37.

[106] A great repository of resources on personal support raising can be found at www.supportraisingsolutions.org.

[107] Ted W. Engstrom, *The Pursuit of Excellence* (Grand Rapids: Zondervan, 1982), 15-16.

CHAPTER 11

[108] Joel Comiskey, *Home Cell Group Explosion* (Houston: Touch Publications, 2000), 34.

[109] Zig Ziglar, *The One Year Daily Insights* (Carol Stream: Tyndale House Publishers, 2009), 266.

[110] Psalm 16:11 and Acts 3:20

[111] University of Florida, "Frequently Asked Questions About Venomous Snakes," *Department of Wildlife Ecology and Conservation*, May 2, 2012, accessed March 13, 2013, http://ufwildlife.ifas.ufl.edu/venomous_snake_faqs.shtml.

[112] David Platt, *Radical* (Colorado Springs: Multnomah Books, 2010), 107.

[113] C.T. Studd referencing Robert Abrahams, "The Night They Burned Shanghai" *Saturday Evening Post*, March 25, 1939, 70, accessed October 8, 2013, http://web.ebscohost.com.

[114] Robert Goldman and Stephen Papson, *Nike Culture: The Sign of Swoosh* (Thousand Oaks: Sage Publications, Inc, 2000), 49.

[115] Napoleon Hill, *Think and Grow Rich* (Meriden: The Ralston Society, 1938), 245.

MISSIONAL COMMUNITY STUDY GUIDE

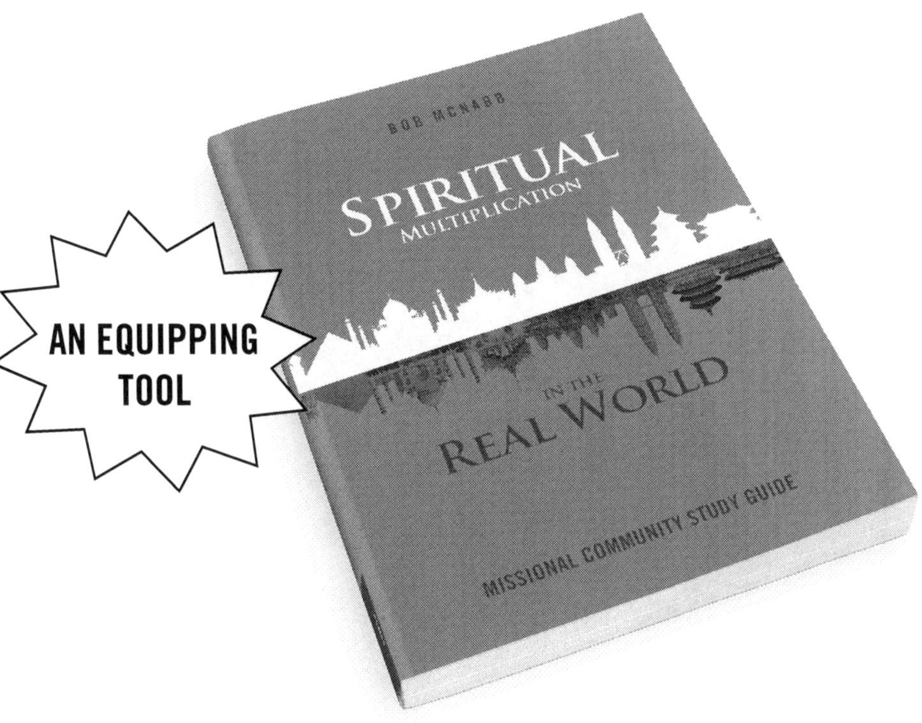

Merely reading about how your group can be a disciple-making team is very different from actually becoming one. Designed for established disciples seeking to be equipped, this *Missional Community Study Guide* is a companion to *Spiritual Multiplication in the Real World* and will help you and your group function as a reproducing *team*. It will direct you week by week into high impact habits, both individually and corporately, propelling you beyond simply making disciples to making disciple-*makers*. This guidebook has proven to be ideal for helping believers who are established in their walks with Christ to become equipped to labor as multipliers in his kingdom.

BULK PRICING AVAILABLE AT SPIRITUALMULTIPLICATION.ORG

FOUNDATIONS:

MISSIONAL COMMUNITY GUIDEBOOK

This resource is designed to lead new believers into missional community and outreach while establishing them in the foundations of the faith. Together, disciples learn how to *grow* in the faith and *bear fruit* as obedient followers of Christ. The *Foundations* guidebook outlines weekly topics such as assurance of salvation, following Christ as Lord, our purpose in life, prayer, the Word, and perseverance in suffering. These and other topics are learned simultaneously with the spiritual disciplines of time alone with God, Bible study, prayer, and Scripture memory. Additionally, crucial Bible interpretation principles and engaging world evangelization facts are presented. *Foundations* is a proven tool to help you solidly ground your disciples in the basics of the Christian life while they learn how to reach out to others as a community.

BULK PRICING AVAILABLE AT SPIRITUALMULTIPLICATION.ORG